Antarctic continent

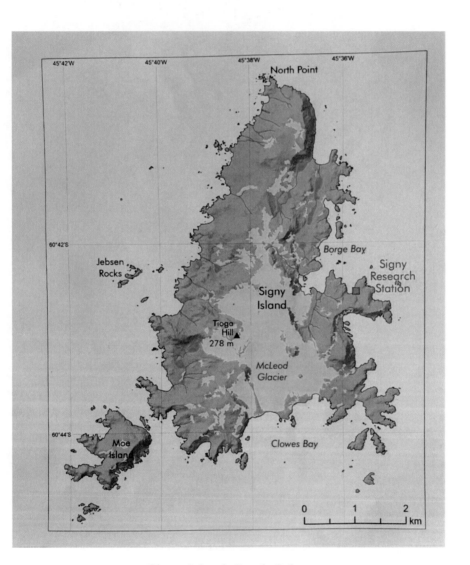

Signy Island, South Orkneys

Antarctic Affair

Fergus O'Gorman

The Harvest Press

First published 2022 by The Harvest Press

ISBN 978-1-8380836-5-6

The author and publishers gratefully acknowledge the support of the County Kildare Decade of Commemorations Committee with the publication of this work.

Dedication

To Alan Sharman – a wonderful companion, who died a few short weeks after we struck camp on Livingston Island; the Signy Islanders who also died; Roger Filer; and those who died at Dion Islands (Stanley Black, David Statham and Geoffrey Stride).

To Dennis 'Tink' Bell and my FIDS companions on the RRS *Shackleton* who died in the course of increasing knowledge of themselves and our understanding of the world around us.

To all the Fids who served loyally since the start of FIDS, and who still do.

And for Sheila, who suffered in relative silence and now keeps the longest silence of all.

We were the fools who could not rest
In the dull earth we left behind
But burned with passion for the South
And drank strange frenzy from the wind.
The world where wise men sit at ease
Fades from our unregretful eyes.
And thus across uncharted Seas
We stagger on our enterprise.

Ernest Shackleton wrote the above lines in the visitors' book on arrival in Punta Arenas, Patagonia, having rescued his men from the *Endurance* on Elephant Island.

Do you recall that sweep of savage splendour,
That land that measures each man at his worth
And feel again in memory, half fierce, half tender,
That brotherhood of men who know the South.

Robert Service, as paraphrased by Ernest Shackleton.

Contents

Preface: Love at First Sight

'Bollocks!' I muttered through clenched teeth as I watched the blood welling through the cracked nail, staining the pristine snow with bright scarlet spots. My ears rang in the frozen air from the crack of the ski binding slamming on my thumb. It was October 1957, my first day in the field in Antarctica on Powell island in the South Orkneys.

It was my first attempt to put on skis and I was struggling to pull on one tight, white silk glove with the other hand. I should never have taken off the gloves in the first place. Even though it was only -12°, I was amazed how quickly one's manual dexterity waned once flesh was exposed to the chilling wind. I grinned sheepishly at the leader, Cecil Scotland. His faint smile of amusement was changing to one of concern. *He must think I'm a stupid clumsy bastard*, I thought. We were just up from the rocky beach where we had been landed and where we had set up the tents for a stay for at least two months. This was to be the first recce ever to Powell Island, to make the first survey and first ever map of the Island.

Derek, the Scot of the survey party guffawed. 'Awch, don't look so worried, you won't die – not just yet, anyway.' Relenting slightly, he added, 'Someone should design a decent binding. If those damn things aren't releasing unasked, they're jammed. All of us have frostbite from the fucking things.' He held up a hand, showing callused and blackened fingertips. 'If someone does produce a decent one, we'll be the last to get them,' was the cynical contribution of Doug, the survey expert. This comment would be heard frequently throughout the next two and a half years.

I turned away, bending down to fumble with the binding and to cover a grimace of pain. What a way to start one's first day. Bloody amateur, belting myself on the thumb. What next? Maybe I'd fall down a crevasse and be done with it. I pulled on new felt mittens over the silk gloves, then added the creamy Beluga whale-skin outer mittens, which hung from a harness around my neck. 'OK?' enquired Cecil casually in his soft Belfast accent. 'Right then, let's be away.'

Across the dark-green sea, flecked with white horses, a line of steep crags rose sheer: sentinels of the strait, warning off intruders with their sharp-fanged reefs of black basalt and marking the easterly end of ninety-mile-long Coronation Island, the principal island in the South Orkney archipelago. To the south, persistent westerly swells, white capped, extended to the horizon and beyond. The next land would be at the head of the Weddell Sea, more than 1,900 miles due south, not far from where Shackleton's *Endurance* had been gripped by pack ice, never to escape. In winter, the view would be solid pack ice to the horizon.

Would it be solid all the way to the continental landmass at 78° south? The South Orkneys would then be on the outermost fringe of Antarctica. Could we walk there without getting our feet wet? I liked to think so. Maybe I'd do it some day; didn't I have all my life to plan such a trip? I glanced at my companions, Cecil, Doug and Derek. Was I barking mad? Could they see this wild whimsy dance across my sweaty face? Would they call up the RRS *Shackleton*, the boat that had dropped me off, and have me removed in chains? No way: they were stuck with me. No rescue possible.

But the men didn't look too worried: they were busy enjoying the break, taking photos and waiting for the new boy to recover. Transfixed by the landscape unfolding endlessly before me, what had gone before – the three-month journey to get here, the excitement of South America, the first iceberg and the fog-shrouded approach to the pack – just melted away. Standing there, feasting my eyes on the icy sea, I felt a stirring that would linger a lifetime. On that day, at that moment, ever bright like the Southern Cross in my memory, began the story of my Antarctic love affair.

Blinking in the glare, I pressed water-laden eyelids to expel their load, which instantly froze to ice across my cheeks. There was an immense feeling of renewal, of rebirth. I'd arrived. But, really, it had all started a long time before.

Introduction: Dublin 1934–57

It began, as so much in my life, with a book – *South with Scott*, written by Robert Falcon Scott's second in command, Edward Evans. Fortunately for him, Evans had been sent back from the South Polar Plateau on the ill-fated British Antarctic Expedition of 1910, together with Tom Crean and William Lashley, as Scott commenced the final push for the South Pole. That stirring tale of explorers and the Great White South led me to take up science as a career. As an undergrad in University College Dublin (UCD), studying biology, I was not to know my first job would be in the Antarctic.

Everything I did as a youth played a part in making that happen. Cycling twelve miles each day back and forth to school from a young age provided the fitness that allowed me to win sprints and jumps in the provincial and national schoolboy championships. My high-jump record at fifteen lasted a decade and a half. My secondary school was O'Connell School, run by the Christian Brothers in North Richmond Street, in Dublin's north inner city, and named after Daniel O'Connell, the great Irish Liberator. My father, with a permanent job in the Civil Service, could just about afford to send my brother Brian and then me to school there. By the time it came to my turn, the Ford jalopy (my father's pride and joy) had to go. So he took the train to work in Dublin Castle (former seat of the British power in Ireland) and I took to my bike.

My friends were all sporty, whether it was endlessly dissecting the last match of football, table or lawn tennis. I was the only one in our group who participated in a solitary sport, in my case athletics, where success or failure was all down to oneself. Few of us had experienced any real isolation, whether physical or mental; even being absorbed by a book was unusual.

5

Comic cuts, as they were called, would do. A quick read of the *Beano*, *Dandy* or *Wizard* would suffice, then out to join up with the group of lads for as long as one was allowed. Back for homework, do as little as possible, just enough to survive the next day in school, then to bed exhausted, sleep, and a new day. No drugs, no drink, no sex (just a few fumbles in the dark) but lots of rock and roll. Once we discovered dancing – the only way that tongue-tied youths could get close to girls – this competed actively with the other sports on offer.

Even in the years of my serious State exams, at fifteen and seventeen, I connived to go dancing. These 'hops', as they were called, were run by various sports clubs scattered across the north side of Dublin, on Wednesdays, Fridays, Saturdays and even Sundays. Sunday activities of any sort were disapproved of by the Church but even more so by my mother, who knew how hard it was any morning, but especially on Mondays, to get me out of bed.

Getting out during the week was always a trial but eventually I developed an escape route that fooled even my mother. Homework was done on the dining-room table, among the competing forces of my older siblings. When it became too much I would retire to my bedroom, which I shared with my brother Brian. I soon found that there was hardly ever any check to see what I was at in the bedroom. It was, after all, on the second floor, and the stairs passed the open door of the kitchen where my mother – the only one who noticed my comings and goings – spent her evenings.

The sitting room, or front room as it was known, was never used for sitting in, but was kept polished and pristine for the occasional important visitor or for visiting aunts and reluctant uncles. My parents thought this demonstrated how far they had come since leaving the inner city and rural Ireland for the leafy suburbia of Clontarf, three miles from the city centre.

I would retire to the bedroom, making sure my mother saw the armful of books, and after a suitable interval, I would cautiously open the right-hand window to peer out at the long narrow garden in case of the unlikely event that my father was doing any gardening. Checking that the neighbours were, similarly, indoors, I would climb out onto the window ledge, gripping the roof guttering for support, close over the window and edge across the ledge until I could grasp the downpipe. Then it was only a matter of a few feet of a slide and I could step onto the flat cement roof of the pantry and down to the ground. A quick sprint down the garden past the lawn and beyond the two Norway spruce – which my father had planted on the day of the declaration of war against Hitler on 3 September 1939 and which he would point out to all visitors – and I would escape to the back lane and freedom.

There I'd spend an hour or two with Sonia, a neighbourhood teenager whose father was something of a celebrity. He was the conductor of the big band at the Royal, the premier theatre for live shows in Dublin. He had brought his wife and daughter from the UK and they had settled just opposite the exit of our back lane. The effectiveness of this exit route was demonstrated one afternoon when I heard my mother entertaining one of the neighbours in the kitchen while I was struggling with algebra in the dining room. She was telling how hard her Fergie was studying for his Intermediate Certificate. 'He goes upstairs most evenings with a pile of books and there's never a peep out of him until bedtime.' That memory still brings a smile to my lips.

Throughout secondary school, I competed at everything, finally settling on athletics; I started rugby only when I left secondary. During the summer holidays, the family decamped to the seaside town of Howth, all of seven miles from where we lived. I spent much of my time there messing around in boats – an important skill to have in the Antarctic, as it turned out.

But first I had to qualify at something or other. I struggled with schoolwork in the last two years. All I wanted to do was sport of whatever kind I could access. I was only seventeen when I sat for the Leaving Cert, which is our final year in school, the gateway to adult life; whether further education or a job.

I tried for the few jobs advertised, but with no luck; I wasn't even called for an interview. It looked like it was going to be a third-level course for me. But what? I had been offered an athletic scholarship in Villa Nova University in the US, but my mother wouldn't contemplate letting me go to America for three years. So I had to try and get into one of the two universities in Dublin, Trinity College or UCD. Trinity was out, for a start: it was Protestant, with Catholics forbidden by the Catholic Archbishop of Dublin from going there! It was going to have to be UCD. However, I had not scored enough points to get an automatic place. I'd have to sit another bloody exam to get in.

I sat it with little hope of succeeding, but much to my surprise I passed. Now I had to find a programme that appealed to me. My interest in birdwatching on Bull Island in Dublin Bay, near my home, suggested biology. But I had never done any biology in school – that was only for girls! I had, however, studied chemistry and scraped a pass, and wasn't maths a science subject? (How I passed maths I'll never know.) With the bare minimum, I was in. I started in UCD in October 1952, which gave me a month to go to the first Catholic Schoolboy Olympics in Manchester and compete in the high jump. My record stood for sixteen years, until 1968.

Despite my inauspicious start, I took to college life like a duck to water. Sports were still high on the list, including rugby, which I had not played before as it was banned by the Christian Brothers as a foreign game! Athletics was okay – after all, an Irishman, Pat O'Callaghan, had won a gold medal in the 1932 Olympics. But it was dance that dominated my free time, which I enjoyed three or four times a week. In those days tennis clubs were the place to go, and where us teens mixed, far from the watchful eye of parents. As regards academics I took them in my stride, enjoying the hands-on lab work but only attending the bare minimum of required lectures. I threw myself into field work, which was all new to me. As long as I passed the end-of-year exams, that was all that mattered.

So here I was, a raw graduate, heading for Antarctica, untrained in every guise; no survival training, virtually no biological research training, no knowledge of seal biology or seal ecology. Ultimately, all my athletic and outdoor activity along with my time in the Boy Scouts played their part in getting me my interview in London for my very first job, as a meteorologist with the Falklands Islands Dependency Survey (FIDS) in Antarctica.

~~~

The Falkland Islands Dependency Survey was the original name for what later became the British Antarctic Survey. Its goal was to support scientific research in the Antarctic, and its members – those who had travelled to the Antarctic and worked on one of the ships or bases – were known as 'Fids'. FIDS was developed after the Second World War, when Britain wanted to prevent Germany from controlling the seas around Cape Horn, the most southern point of South America. The Falkland Islands was the closest area – 300 miles, more or less – where Britain could maintain a naval force and there was an English-speaking community. Most of the population was made up of ex-Shetland Islanders who had colonised the Falklands in the nineteenth century to exploit the massive seal and whale populations. These

9

had been virtually wiped out by the end of the century and the Kelpers, as the locals were known, depended on sheep farming on the islands.

FIDS recruited qualified geographers and surveyors, geologists and glaciologists, geophysicists and astrophysicists, as well as support staff including cooks, medics, mountaineers and meteorologists, diesel mechanics and radio operators. We also had 'gash hands' who did everything on base, including maintenance and cleaning, and if you talked to them nicely they might even do your washing and ironing! At the time, these were all men and it wasn't until 1980 that the first female operational staff appeared in Antarctica.

The director of FIDS from 1958 to 1973 was Vivian Fuchs, who was in the Antarctic having organised the second attempt at crossing the Antarctic continent. Ernest Shackleton had tried in 1914 to do it, and failed. Fuchs joined with Sir Edmund Hillary to make the first successful crossing. The London HQ was run by Sir Raymond Priestley. He had been down South as a geologist with Robert Falcon Scott in 1911 and survived to join Shackleton's failed trans-Antarctic expedition of 1914–16. The small staff included Bill Sloman, the personnel officer, Frank Elliott, a veteran of the FIDS operation down South, and 'Anne' Todd, who was long term in the office and could answer all and any questions while looking after the few young women who provided secretarial support.

The HQ was a small office in London's Millbank. Here, staff were recruited for the International Geophysical Year (IGY) Scientific Programme, which was focused on geographical exploration and mapping, as very little of Antarctica had been mapped at that time. The possibility of finding valuable resources of oil or minerals before other national expeditions became an overriding objective. In the early 1950s the

International Scientific Union, a global coming together of scientists, had proposed the IGY. It was to take place in 1957–8 but ran on into 1959. This led to a surge of new bases in the Antarctic. Britain expanded its bases and, by 1959, thirty-three bases had been opened by IGY nations, mostly scattered around the Antarctic Peninsula. By 1961 it was down to nineteen, with one extra at the head of the Weddell Sea at Halley Bay. As a consequence of IGY, in 1959 twelve nations signed the Antarctic Treaty, which declared that Antarctica would only be used for peaceful purposes and to develop science programmes to benefit all mankind.

Having applied to FIDS for a job as a glaciologist (despite knowing practically nothing about the subject), I was called for an interview as a meteorologist, about which I knew even less, in August 1957. My main role was to collect data for a global network of weather systems. After arriving overnight from Dublin on the *Princess Maud*, the lumbering ferry that plied the Irish Sea between Dublin and Holyhead, I caught the night train to Euston Station in London, arriving at 6.30 am. I soaked up a traditional British breakfast of bangers and beans on arrival, then headed for Millbank on the River Thames, where I ended up in a room with eight other young men, waiting to be interviewed.

The interviews began and, when the queue was down to three of us, I plucked up the courage to speak to the emerging candidate in front of me. 'What was it like?' I enquired. 'Fucking awful,' was the reply. *Oh, well, I've had a free trip to London*, I mused to myself.

I was last in. Operations officer Frank Elliott, wearing a well-worn suit, introduced himself. Personnel officer Bill Sloman, in contrast, was spick and span, with his gold cufflinks showing, his pin-striped suit just off the peg. Frank started by reading my CV and asking me to expand on the information

11

therein. I gave my answer and waited for a follow-on grilling. Into the pause, Bill interjected: 'You're a Roman Catholic, aren't you?' I gulped. 'Yes,' I acknowledged. 'The rest of the chaps will be Protestants,' Bill stated in his Welsh accent, his face stiff. 'Will that be a problem?'

I was caught on the hop with the sudden change of direction. Instinctively, I knew this would be a turning point. I looked Bill straight in the eye. 'No, not at all. Some of my best friends are Welsh,' I responded with a half grin. Frank spluttered and coughed into his hand, his eyes glistening with suppressed laughter. Bill beamed. 'I've known a few Paddies in my day. They weren't all bad muckers.' He paused. 'By the way, we have a job for a biologist. Would you be interested?'

'Yes,' I stammered, a wide grin spreading across my face. They smiled, all of us happy with Bill's decision. 'You'll have to have another interview, of course: a professional one, with Dr Frazer, the whale man, at the British Museum. Come into the office in the morning and ask Anne to arrange it.' We stood up and shook hands. I left, floating.

The following morning I made my way to the Natural History Museum in South Kensington, where I found Dr Frazer deep in the basement, surrounded by seal skulls. I was greeted with 'I'm making a cup of tea, would you be interested?' Naturally I said yes. He talked about his collection of skulls and, twenty minutes later, said, 'I'm supposed to be interviewing you for a job.' He paused, a frown on his face. 'What does a Leopard seal look like?' he asked. 'Long and snaky,' I replied. 'You'll do,' he said with a grin.

Having passed these initial hurdles, I was sent to the Commonwealth and Colonial Office to have a medical and psychological examination. While the chief medical officer was jotting down my personal details, I noticed he was wearing a Cambridge rugby tie. As I'd only just read the report of the annual

Oxford vs Cambridge match in Twickenham in *The Times* while I was in the waiting room, I immediately and cunningly asked if he had been there. Following the discovery that I was a keen player of the game, my medical consisted of checking my eyesight, looking at my teeth, taking my blood pressure and discussing why Oxford had won and not Cambridge. The encounter ended with him saying, 'You'll do just fine.' Obviously, rugger types were fully prepared psychologically for the stresses of Antarctic life!

Having survived my first sojourn to London, I was delighted to be offered my first ever job, not as assistant meteorologist but as a research biologist, no less. I rushed back to Dublin to give my family the good news and was shocked when my mother burst into tears. Having already forbidden me to take up that athletics scholarship to the US , she was now still going to lose her 'Fergie Óg', her youngest child, at twenty-one, for three years. She wondered how I would survive the hazards of Antarctica. Not that she knew what those hazards were; she was having difficulty finding Antarctica on the map. It was down there somewhere, she said, as she pointed to the blank space on the bottom of our family globe.

The Journey South

At the end of July I packed up my climbing boots and my joke of an anorak (it wasn't even warm enough for an Irish summer) and headed to my good friend Tom Earls, in Shepherd's Bush in London, the geologist from college who had alerted me to the FIDS ad. Once I turned up in the FIDS office Anne Todd took me under her wing, arranging for me to be paid per diem until I officially started on the job on 1 September.

I scurried around London that early autumn of 1957, trying to acquire the equipment I thought I might need to carry out my research. Everything I had ordered went to the Crown Agents who handled all FIDS business outside the UK. There was so much stuff the crates were labelled BASE O'Gorman, causing much hilarity when it arrived at the Signy Island base in the South Orkneys.

I never had a thought about the hazards I was going to be exposed to. Nor was there any suggestion that survival training was essential; it was never even mentioned. So I stepped onto the RRS *Shackleton* on 1 October 1957 without any qualms or forebodings, only a rush of excitement and adrenaline. At last it was happening.

I had no feelings of panic or fear of the unknown, no thoughts as I waved to my parents on the dock that I might never see them, or Ireland, again. I knew nothing of the Fids who had died in the past: four up to that point and, eventually, twenty-six in all, six of them while I was there. I don't think it would have made any difference; I was twenty-one and felt invincible. Twenty-eight new boys boarded the RRS *Shackleton* on that day. These were a sprinkling of other sciences: astrophysics, geology, geographers but most were newly minted meteorologists, as well as diesel mechanics, radio operators and 'gash' hands (field assistants and such like). All but two of us would survive the multiple hazards of the Antarctic before returning home on the *John Biscoe* in April 1960.

Surviving two years and seven months was no mean feat.

The passage from Southampton to Montevideo was not without incident. By the end of the first day, when we got to the Bay of Biscay, the whole crew had come down with Asian flu. They all became bed-ridden, with the exception of the officers, who were upstairs with us. So we, the explorers, had to take over and run the ship for twenty-eight days, which was an unexpected amount of very hard work.

The boys came from every corner of the UK, but I was the only Paddy and was never allowed to forget it. All of us were in our twenties or early thirties. Unlike most of them, I had not done compulsory national service after school, which gave them a huge advantage over me. They were used to living cheek by jowl in cramped conditions with a melange of young men of diverse cultural and educational backgrounds. Linguistically, they appeared to me to be from outer space. I had never heard such a range of accents, from Cockney to Scouse, to Welsh and Scots. It took me the first month to understand the basics of their English language.

Despite spending so much time together, I learnt surprisingly little about their family backgrounds or their life before they became Fids, perhaps because I didn't drink and so didn't spend much of my time in the bar. I also spent a lot of time preparing for my role by reading the voluminous FIDS publications or recording the oceanic birds with Alan Sharman, the only other keen birdwatcher. I did, however, become friendly with George White, a native of Wotton-under-Edge in Gloucestershire, a diesel mechanic and the ultimate anti-establishment man. Nothing was right in Britain. We used to enjoy listening to him lambast some icon of government or FIDS, all of whom were intent on making life unbearable for a decent working man like himself.

~~~

Of the twenty-eight new 'explorers' on the *Shackleton*, only the two medics had ever come in contact with death. Yet their only concern was alerting us to the dangers of STDs, herding us together for a talk on 'the clap' and how you could die of syphilis. I had never heard of either, despite having spent four years studying biology in Dublin, so when the docs regaled us about the dangers of unprotected sex, my mouth hung open. As a 21-year-old Irish Catholic virgin, I was never going there. I was shocked to the core. That attitude was reinforced when one of the Fids came back on board in Monte after an all-nighter and showed off his red and raw manhood for all to admire. He told us how many times he'd had it off with the ladies of the night, until he'd run out of money. Needless to say, he got a dose of the clap, and when we got to Port Stanley in the Falklands he was put on the next boat home.

~~~

For most of us Fids, the stopover in Montevideo (the only one en route to the Falkland Islands) was our first contact with the Spanish language. Those who dared leave the ship stayed with a Mrs Hawkins in Pocitos, on the beach, a stone's throw from the Plaza de Independencia, the heart of the city. (Only once did a Fid winter in Montevideo, at least at HMG's expense. He met and married a Uruguayan who spoke English with a County Mayo accent, but that's another story.) It was in Montevideo that I first experienced a nightclub: to be surrounded by a multitude of young women, all wanting to take me home, was mindboggling. One insisted on sitting on my knee while she ordered a drink. After she bounced up and down on my lap multiple times, I thought my pants would explode. Escape was the only solution. I burst out onto the sidewalk and hurriedly got a taxi back to the ship.

The next morning I was informed by the shipping agents, McLean & Stapleton, that I should help two new arrivals who had just flown in from London and would show up in the next hour or so. I guessed that they must be VIPs, as only the brass got to fly from Europe. They were Professor Jim Cragg, from the University of Newcastle, and Llewellyn Chantor, the foreign correspondent of the *Daily Telegraph*.

I alerted the bridge to their imminent arrival and within an hour they were debouched from a taxi alongside. They were ushered on board and taken up to the bridge, while their overloaded luggage was man-hauled on board by a deckhand. The skipper, Norman Brown, welcomed them on board and introduced me as the Fid who would help them settle in and look after them until they arrived in Port Stanley.

After Clive, the purser, had sorted out their cabins, I introduced them to the other Fids in our saloon and we learnt why they were joining us. It turned out the professor was doing a recce with the objective of setting up a biology programme for FIDS. That was right up my alley. Llewellyn, the *Daily Telegraph* man (known as Lew) was there to report on how and why HMG was manning eleven bases in Antarctica, and to demonstrate how important the work was, geopolitically and scientifically. They quizzed me up and down as to how an Irishman, and a republican to boot (Ireland had declared a republic ten years previously), had come to be on a very British expedition. In the process, they discovered that it had been my birthday a couple of days earlier. I was all of twenty-two!

Lew proposed, with the agreement of Prof. Jim, to take me out to celebrate. We walked up to the main plaza and into the Hotel Nogaro, the best such establishment in the city. Lew led the way. We were ushered to a table decked with a white tablecloth and row upon row of cutlery. This was another first for me. I had never been to a hotel or restaurant for a meal. We were seated by a frock-coated waiter wearing gloves, who insisted on unfolding the starched white napkin on a side plate and putting it on my lap. I was totally embarrassed, blushing to the roots of my hair. Lew grinned while the Prof smiled encouragingly.

The waiter returned, pushing a trolley stacked high with various sorts of bread, none of which I recognised. I took a slice with large holes in it, and wondered why we were being offered slices from a failed loaf; why didn't the baker just throw it out? It was now 8 pm. We usually ate at 5.30 pm on the *Shack* and I was starving. I proceeded to slap butter on the bread and gulp it down.

Instantly, the waiter and trolley reappeared, offering more bread. Before grabbing another slice, I glanced up and caught the Prof's eye. He was shaking his head imperceptibly, warning me not to take any more.

When I turned to say 'No' to the bread waiter, he had been replaced by another with a trolley filled with little bowls. Do I drink it? No, go with the small spoon as the Prof and Lew were doing. It tasted slightly astringent. Surreptitiously, I fished out a hard bit on my finger and stared. My God! Being a biologist helped. It was part of an isopod, a tiny shrimp-like creature, which I had found during many a sea-pool crawl around Dublin Bay.

I had never eaten seafood. My mother detested creepy crawlies and the only wildlife we ate was wild rabbit or not-so-wild chicken and, of course, fish on Fridays, compulsory for us God-fearing Catholic Irish. Even then, salvation was limited as it was dried salted cod that came from Grimsby. It had to be soaked overnight to make it pliable and to get rid of some of the salt before boiling.

Now I was being offered a sludge of ground-up shrimps. Would I follow the two Brits opposite me and wolf it down? Not bloody likely! I waited for the glove to appear and whisk it away. My companions, who were rabbiting on about British politics, smiled and carried on.

Before we pulled away from the dock in Montevideo late in the afternoon the next day, most of the lads went last-minute shopping while I took a taxi to the beach at Pocitos. There I lay in the sun, shirt off, wondering how long it would be before I could do this again as I tried to get my head around the prospect of spending two and a half years in Antarctica. I reckoned there would be no sunbathing in the Falkland Islands. The couple of hours spent soaking up the sun revived me and I left Pocitos feeling the afterglow, little thinking I'd be back on the same beach in the not-too-distant future.

~~~

We were headed to the Falkland Islands, our launching pad for the Antarctic. From there we would go to South Georgia, a wild and beautiful sub-Antarctic island and the headquarters of the whaling industry. Then we would proceed to the South Orkneys, where I would get off and join a summer survey party on Powell Island to the east. The RRS *Shackleton* would head for the South Shetlands and the Antarctic Peninsula to relieve the existing bases by renewing supplies, depositing new staff and collecting those who were heading home.

Leaving Buenos Aires with the remains of the German battle cruiser *Graf Spree* – scuttled during the Battle of the River Plate in 1939 – still showing above the waves, we headed down the long coast of Patagonia to the Falkland Islands, a four-day trip in those days. Turning right, we pushed past Mar del Plata, finally leaving the great estuary behind, and headed south. At last we were on our way, after nearly three weeks of hanging round in Montevideo.

Lots of heavy weather but little excitement except for a vast increase in the number of Albatross heading south – until we saw our first iceberg.

Seeing one's first iceberg was a moment of personal history, imprinted forever on the subconscious. We were out from the Falkland Islands, ploughing southeast through the long rollers of the frightful fifties when we saw it. My diary entry said laconically: *November 12th at 14.30 we saw our first iceberg. Small by all accounts but quite impressive.* The entry fails to express the flush of excitement when the shout went up: 'Berg on the starboard bow!' or the frenzied rush to grab cameras, binoculars and duffle coat, all in one motion, as if it were merely a fleeting illusion and not a substantial chunk of ice ploughing its own furrow to destruction further north. We stood grouped on the fo'c'sle, or draped over the flying bridge, and soaked up the sight. Among the cacophony of camera clicks, it was difficult to comprehend that we were at the same latitude as Liverpool.

~~~

Antarctica, to most people, is just a blob on the map: a rather large blob but, nonetheless, a white, indefinable place. For those of us brought up on adventure stories, it's the scene of Scott of the Antarctic, naval officer, martinet, full of glorious heroism and stupid ambition. Maybe we even think of 'Uncle' Bill Wilson, the gentle naturalist who died with Scott in that organisational fiasco returning from the South Pole.

Or we may think of the boss, Ernest Shackleton, whose leadership drove a small open boat across the Antarctic seas to rescue his shipwrecked men. Shackleton was also an Irishman: he was born and spent his early life in Co. Kildare. Naturally, that is not the reason that in Antarctic exploring circles Shackleton is more highly regarded nowadays than Scott. A companion of both, Sir Raymond Priestley, whom I met near the end of his days, gave me the strong impression that even he would agree. He was reluctant to be drawn on Scott; after all, you do not run down a nation's heroes, even by implication. 'But the Boss, now he was a man!'

Few have felt the chilling, piercing glow of the Antarctic sunrise flashing in pastel blues and greens from crystal clusters of star-shaped snow, which penetrate one's winter wear to lodge in that area above the diaphragm where one is wont to harbour gladness or sadness, pain or love. Oh, that terrible beauty that ricochets into one's very soul and lodges in the heart, lingering for long days before slowly diffusing into one's subconscious. Years later it can be brought back into sharp focus when a thought, an act, or a word triggers that mental synapse marked love, flooding the mind in a rush of swirling, drowning images of days gone by, of instances remote in time and place, which flash across the mind like the starbursts of the Aurora Australis.

Of course I did not understand, even vaguely, the brooding menace of Antarctica's immensity. However, I was aware of some vague, unconscious, perception of what lay ahead; of not merely the physical but also the emotional immensity of the world I was entering into.

Antarctica is a massive continent. It covers an area of five and a half million square miles across the southern roof of the world. Most of the land mass is south of 70°, except for the mountainous Antarctic Peninsula, which stretches up to meet its towering cousin, the Andes, just failing to do so by a mere 600 miles or so. Here, the Drake Passage, dreaded as much by the single-handers today as by the clipper men of yore, separates Cape Horn in the north from Hope Bay in the south, but cannot prevent the Antarctic's fingertips from protruding through its storm-capped waves in a series of islands stretching from the South Shetlands through the South Orkneys and South Sandwich to South Georgia.

Biologically, Antarctica extends even further north, to 50° latitude, where the Antarctic Convergence occurs. This is where the frigid Antarctic currents meet the warmer and more saline sub-Antarctic waters. Of course, warmer is relative. The sub-Antarctic water is only degrees warmer than that of the Antarctic, which brings it up a meagre 2° in winter and 6° in summer. Even those used to swimming in the cold temperate waters of northern Europe, where our sea temperatures vary on average between 14° and 18°, would find the difference a bit much to take.

Despite the chilly waters, swimming is a fairly regular occurrence on the Falkland Islands, which at latitude 52° feel the bite of the cold currents sweeping through Drake's Passage and around Cape Horn.

The reason we don't see bergs at that latitude in Europe is that the Arctic, straddling the North Pole, is a minuscule cold region in comparison with the Antarctic. True, it covers a fair enough area – about five million square miles of more or less permanent ice, as well as the Greenland ice cap, which covers around 700,000 square miles – but, except for Greenland, this is all floating sea ice, a mere fifteen to twenty feet thick at its greatest.

The Antarctic is a different kettle of fish. As well as five and a half million square miles of permanently ice-covered continent, which is two and a half times the size of Europe, it has ice shelves that extend out from the continent. These floating layers of hard-packed ice cover 800,000 square miles. The continental ice cap varies between 6,500 and 8,200 feet thick on average. Its maximum depth is an incredible 11,000 feet. The ice that covers the continent forms a massive load and amounts to twenty-nine million cubic kilometres – more than 90 per cent of the Earth's total ice, and 3 per cent of all the Earth's water.

This may sound like an insignificant fraction, but if the Antarctic ice should melt – and it has been suggested by some environmentalists that is what is happening according to climate change experts – the world's sea level would rise 200 feet, which, naturally, would flood a large part of the inhabited coastlines. Of course, if this weight of ice were removed, we would expect some readjustment upwards to compensate for the removal, somewhat like the effect of taking your hand off a sponge. The Antarctic and the surrounding ocean floors would rise, but only by seventy feet. So even a partial melt would lead to a devastating rise in the world's seas.

In Antarctica, a dramatic change seems unlikely but not impossible. Annually, a fantastic amount of snow falls in the region. It's been worked out that one to two million, million tonnes of snow are added each year (that extra million is not a misprint), which squeezes out the underlying layers like toothpaste out of a tube; these slowly flow down to the seas in multitudinous glaciers. The glaciers push off from the shoreline like gigantic ice lollies, whose ends break off to form the myriad bergs that jostle each other like monstrous, glistening ghosts at an aquatic dodgems. Bergs a hundred miles long and twenty miles wide have been met and mapped in the Antarctic oceans. As well as the continental ice cap and the shelf ice masses, there is also the pack ice to take into account. Even in summer this frozen sea never fully melts. It probably only reduces to 50 per cent of its winter area. In winter, the pack ice doubles the area of the Antarctic Ice.

It also has an impact on the weather. At the South Pole, the average annual temperature is an incredible -51°C! However, the highest average monthly temperature is much higher, climbing to -25°C. Over the past twenty-five years, climate change has been recognized by most of the world's scientists as real: an increasing danger to a sustainable planet for the world population projected to increase from seven and a half billion to close to ten billion by

2050. The Arctic Ocean could be ice free by then, and the Antarctic ice much reduced, with inundation of coastlines on a global scale, changing food cycles and bringing even more starvation in the developing world than at present.

~~~

The *Shackleton* was heading for the Falkland Islands, technically at the same latitude as Liverpool but a world apart. The Falklands are a cold and windswept series of islands, 300 miles from Cape Horn. In those days the population was around 2500, the majority of whom lived in the capital, Port Stanley.

The first time I saw an Albatross, I was initially disappointed. Having read Coleridge's *The Rime of the Ancient Mariner*, in my mind's eye it should have been massive, majestic even, with an evil glint in its eye and a fearsome hook to its bill, capable of shearing the flesh from the bone, or plucking out an eye as efficiently as an Egyptian vulture. So its sweeping arrival, just north of the Equator – on ultra-thin wings, ends drooping, demonstrating the gravitational pull on such delicate structures – was seen from afar with great excitement. As it sped closer, with hardly a twitch of a feather, but gliding down on the wave-generated wind, it seemed to diminish.

It glided downwind, banking left and rising on the updraft from an enormous wave, going up fifty feet and then rushing down with increasing speed so that within seconds it seemed the bird was alongside the ship, as the *Shackleton* plunged through the same wave, causing clouds of spray from the bow to crash into the reinforced glass panels on the bridge. For a few seconds, we were connected eye to eye. This was no common-or-garden homegrown gull but a fiercely independent, solitary denizen of the ocean depths, delicately designed for its elegance.

25

It must have been twice as big as any gull, and it was one of the smaller Albatrosses – the Black-Browed – black on the wings, and glowing white elsewhere except for a quizzical black eyebrow and even blacker eyes. Its beauty, its wildness, pierced my soul. Ever after, all Albatrosses, of whatever species, had to measure up to that first meeting. But even the glories of the great Wandering Albatross, nearly twice as large, with wings extending to two human body lengths, could not compare with that first enthralling encounter.

Soon, Albatrosses were a constant companion to the ship. All they needed was heavy weather, preferably something approaching a gale. It became obvious how energy efficient they were. Weren't they flying around the world, circumnavigating the Southern Ocean continuously (or so my mate Lance Tickell intimated), followed by the Giant Petrels, which were being ringed as chicks at Signy Island? And hadn't they been turning up downwind (and dead) in South Africa, Australia and New Zealand? As soon as rings were reported from South America, probably from Tierra del Fuego, we would have conclusive proof.

I still remember the thrill when the shout came over the ship's Tannoy: 'Penguins! Off the port bow!' Everyone rushed to the port rail. There they were – little black, well-stuffed cigars porpoising (as it's called) through the waves. Just a flash of a black body, then under, then a two- to three-second pause before another brief reprise. I dashed down to my cabin. Damn! As usual, just when you want your binoculars you don't have them. I bounced back on deck. Now the party was made up of twenty or thirty, but how do you count penguins accurately when they are each coming up and going down at different rhythms? Am I counting the same one twice? Ten times?

That first occasion my notebook merely records *11–30 penguins –Adélies???*
20–30??

We were halfway down the Argentine coast, probably not far from
Peninsula Valdés which, today, is regarded as a wonder of the natural world
and is a World Heritage Site. Back then, no one had ever heard of it, at least
outside of a few Buenos Aires naturalists. The famous Angel Cabrera two-
volume work *Mamiferos del America del Sur* (*The Mammals of South
America*) doesn't even mention it in the index. Yet this is one of the great
places for seals and whales – maybe the greatest in Argentina.

I also remember the images in *National Geographic* of Killer whales
rushing onto Valdés' beaches to take the Fur seals lying there. After being
stranded by the retreating wave, they would roll over and down the beach
until lifted by the next incoming breaker. These were amazing pictures of a
world we biologists knew nothing about. David Attenborough, in his first
thirteen-hour television series, *Life on Earth*, in 1979, captured underwater
shots of a pod of Killer whales working this area, killing seals. They were
amazing pictures and the image always reminds me of the cartoon of two
Killer whales looking at two divers in rubber suits. One says to the other,
'They're really quite nice once you pull off the rubber wrapping.'

The penguins flashed into the air again, with heads down they met the
oncoming wave and in a millisecond their dark shape disappeared beneath.
It was a memorable glimpse of what was to come.

Port Stanley, Falkland Islands

The *Shack* made quite an impact on arrival – mostly involving the pier. A number of people were knocked off their feet and it made a significant dent in the jetty. As you can imagine, Captain Norman Brown was not popular with the brass waiting to greet us. (A further incident a month later, involving a near sinking in the ice in the Scotia Sea, heralded an end to Norman's time in the Antarctic.)

The FIDS office, set up in 1945, was the HQ for all the operations in the Antarctic, and reported directly to HQ in London. At the time of our arrival the Falklands capital, Port Stanley, was a one-horse town and home to mostly Shetland Islanders who had migrated there in the early nineteenth century, to make their fortunes by killing Fur seals. When the seals were wiped out they started the onslaught on the great whales, which were on their last legs when we arrived in 1957. By the mid-sixties they were virtually extinct and the whaling industry, headquartered on South Georgia, also collapsed.

We had hardly tied up to the jetty when we were engulfed by a mass of Kelpers (the nickname given to Falkland islanders) wanting to hear a new voice, see a new face, talk about what was happening in the outside world, especially 'at home' in the UK, where most of the younger ones had never been.

Charles Darwin, who arrived in 1834 on HMS *Beagle*, thought it was about half the size of Ireland but, at 4,700 square miles, it is less than 15 per cent of the whole island of Ireland. The islands are firmly in the cold, temperate zone of the South Atlantic, and are well known as a place with not enough trees to hang a man nor soil to bury him, to quote the Roundhead general Edmund Ludlow, who pillaged the bleak landscape of the Burren in the West of Ireland in the seventeenth century.

Even if seedlings emerged, they hardly had put their heads above the parapet when the ferocious jaws of the multitudinous sheep would pluck them out in order to add to the Kelpers' only source of wealth. We were astonished to discover that a pound of sheep meat cost only four old pence!

It is hard to believe that in 1982 Britain and Argentina fought a war for the Falklands resulting in the deaths of so many young soldiers and airmen on both sides. In 1767 Fr Sebastian Villanueva described the new Spanish settlement in the East Falklands as 'this unhappy desert'. 'Not a tree, not a shrub is there. And incessant gales and the stormy seas added to the barren cruelty of the soil' would not encourage anyone to settle there, much less fight over it. In the early 1900s Viscount Bryce wrote that the Falklands were 'a land without form or expression' and that he'd never seen 'any inhabited spot that seemed so entirely desolate and solitary'.

This desolate archipelago consists of two large islands, East and West Falklands, and nearly 200 others scattered over an area of 120 x 60 miles. Patagonia is 300 miles away as the Albatross glides, and Tierra del Fuego and the entrance to the Straits of Magellan, such a magnet to navigators of yore, are 250 miles away. Ecologically, the Falklands area is equally impoverished. Only a stone's throw from the notorious Cape Horn, it does not encourage even the Tierra del Fuegian insects to leave the comfort of their beech forest to live there. However, birds and marine mammals are a different matter. Both have an insulating layer, one of feathers and the other of blubber, to keep out the cold, making the Falklands a delight.

Our first day in Port Stanley was spent mooching around, seeing the sights (very few) and getting acclimatised to the constant wind coming from Cape Horn or parts south. By the first evening, we Fids had done everything Stanley had to offer the new tourist and were wondering where to next.

That's when Sadie, the senior girl at the FIDS office, took pity on some of us. We were invited to tea and buns in her house, which was close to the FIDS office where she worked. There we met Stanley Greene, FIDS secretary, who ran the operation out of Port Stanley, and the rest of the staff, all female. A few locals were included, so we Fids got a feeling of what talent was available.

We were to spend ten days in Stanley, loading stores and getting kitted out with our Antarctic gear in between the constant parties, which seemed to start after breakfast every day and run until well after midnight. The arrival of a horde of hot young males into the isolated population didn't happen every day, and the locals made the most of it. One of my most endearing memories of Stanley was being woken up late one night, half a dozen very dead Steamer Ducks having been dumped on my chest by a gaggle of well-oiled collectors. 'Here you are then. The bloody British Museum will be delighted with this lot. Provided you stuff them properly.' This comment led to several suggestions as to where and how they might be stuffed, in true services fashion.

~~~

On that first visit, on the few days when the sun shone and the lashing, wind-driven rain subsided to mere showers, the gently rolling grasslands around Port Stanley resembled England's south-coast downs, but with subtle differences. The long, lank grasses didn't look like any that I had studied in my home meadows. Not a bird was the same, unless I included the Oystercatcher probing the sea-wrack at the edge of the tide. Instead of being black and white with a red bill and legs, as in Europe, this one was black all over; but it was still an Oystercatcher. The tiny, courageous tussock bird was determined to share my lunch, to the extent of darting on to the toe of my boot, and then my knee. Making a quick calculation, volume for volume, crumbs were the answer. As two of the birds would fit comfortably in the palm of my hand, a few crumbs would do.

I was glad the evil-eyed caracara was a bit shyer. He was standing off three or four yards, his piercing glance fixated on my hand-to-mouth action. On to the paper bag, up to the mouth; bite off a bit, back in the bag. Up with the binoculars, to peer eyeball to eyeball into the iris of his mind. He lifted his viciously hooked bill up and down as he hopped with a fast one-two beat around me. A crick-of-the-neck-making exercise, as I wasn't sure if or when a hop would land too close for comfort. I had been told to watch out for 'those vicious bastards' by a local Kelper. It was nerve-wracking to be this close to a large bird of prey for the very first time; especially one who was eyeing me and my lunch with desire. The closest I had ever been was a hundred feet away from nesting peregrines in the Wicklow hills. Peregrines are less than half the size of the caracara, which can weigh up to one and a half kilos.

I pulled out my notebook and made a few notes. My fumbling in my rucksack brought the caracara a hop too close. Quite suddenly I was staring into its black, glistening eye and wicked bill, not one foot away. My nerve broke and I swung my father's binoculars – the only thing of his that I had – at the scavenger. Unflustered, the caracara settled down out of reach. The pair of binoculars, on the other hand, reached the end of its rotation and, with the cracking of its ancient leather strap, disappeared into a nearby tussock. A four-letter roar followed. Even that didn't disturb my silent scavenger.

If I got up and pursued the binoculars, my lunch would be no more. Keeping my eyes on my predator, I returned all the edibles to the sack. Was he capable of stealing my rucksack? Surely not. However, I hooked it over my shoulder and took the two paces to the tussock. One hop and I was not alone. I bent down, driving my right arm into the two-foot mound of matted, spiky, grass-like plants, turning my head, closing my right eye and pressing my cheek into the spikes while I felt around the innards. I squinted sideways to keep my only operational eye on the antics of my caracara friend. Now my eyes were level with his black glare and he was only a foot away. I hastily grabbed the binoculars and stood up, feeling safe at last.

I'd had enough of this eyeball-to-eyeball contest; lunch would have to wait. I bustled through the heaps of tussock grass. As I glanced over my shoulder, sure enough, my caracara was keeping pace, hopping from tussock top to tussock top. How would I ever get rid of him? I increased my pace. He flapped between hops. By this stage, I was nearly running – not too easy with a loaded rucksack.

Finally, I came to a gate opening onto the road back to Stanley. The caracara was perched on the gatepost, watching my progress. Better not sit down yet; I could suffer the hunger a bit longer. This was a lunch to remember!

The arrival of a royal research ship in Stanley was greatly welcomed by the locals. After all, there were just 1,500 people in Stanley, with another 1,000 scattered throughout the islands. The arrival of a ship packed with young men was an event not to be missed. Even the men in the pubs welcomed new voices, new topics and a touch of the outside world, if only for a week or two. It was all very well getting the news from the BBC, but the reception could be atrocious, and the Falkland Island radio news was simply a pale reflection of what was going on in the wider world, as well as being repetitive. The fact that 'the Paris of the South' – sophisticated Buenos Aires – was only up the way, four days by boat, meant nothing. *They were only bloody Argies, speaking broken English, if any. And foreign. Mixed with all them Eye-ties (Italians) who fought the Brits during the war. And they had the cheek, the bloody cheek, to call the Falklands the Mal-vin-as, whatever that meant.* This attitude led to the bloody Falklands War in 1982, in which nearly 1,000 soldiers died.

For those few days after the arrival of a ship, Port Stanley came alive, and for the Fids it was one long party. Coffee mornings and afternoon tea and buns in various houses and flats were legion, followed by pub evenings and late-night snacks. There was no doubt that the way to a young man's heart was through his stomach and after months of ship food, any homemade offerings were lapped up. For most of us, however, the dances were the highlight. At these you could mingle with the opposite sex without embarrassment or blushes. Touching, whether hands, shoulders, back, knees, thighs or bottoms, was merely part of the required skill for the local dances. The fumble in the dark, the hot lips and pounding pulse, followed by the fatigued trudge back to the *Shack* – ah, dem were the days! While those nights have faded deep into the memory bank, one such incident stands out, remembered as if it was yesterday.

'What's this about you and the gov's daughter?' enquired Jim Shirtcliffe with a raised eyebrow. He had come down south to be one of the builders putting up new bases and repairing old ones. He was a good six feet and muscular, bulging out of his shirt and pants. He had quite an eye for the girls and they for him. I looked at him, innocence personified. All I had done was my dancing thing. The fact that I could get around the floor as fast as greased lightning, my breakneck speed sweeping all in front of me, as well as doing swirls, did not go unnoticed amongst the Stanley ladies, attached and otherwise.

Being different, I've always found, helps you stand out from the crowd, and a message soon arrived on board inviting myself and Jim to have dinner with the Governor, Sir Edwin Arrowsmith, and his wife, Lady Arrowsmith. Sir Edwin was the Colonial Office's 'man on the ground', supposedly with his finger on the geopolitical pulse of the region. What I didn't know was that his two teenage daughters, fresh out of Blighty, would also be present. We had to dress up for the first time since leaving Southampton. I put on my only suit and tie. Jim was much more casually dressed. We walked down from the jetty to the front gates of the governor's mansion.

The door opened at the first ring of the bell. We were met by a befrocked maid who ushered us into the drawing room where the Governor and Lady Arrowsmith were ensconced, with their two daughters bringing up the rear. I hadn't met them before; they had recently arrived on the MV *Darwin* from Montevideo, to spend the summer in this outpost of the Empire. The elder, Susan, aged nineteen, had just finished at Roedean. With her sister, Jennifer, aged seventeen, she was greeting their release with enthusiasm.

Needless to say, I was smitten. I had difficulty keeping my eyes off Susan, but dinner went off without a hitch. To my relief, Sir Edwin announced that he and her ladyship would withdraw after tea was served. No sooner had they gone than we four withdrew to the sitting room. Jim and Jennifer spread themselves out on the sofa, which forced Susan onto the sofa's arm facing inwards. Of course, I had to join her there.

When the conversation got around to party tricks, I had to admit I didn't have one, whereupon Jim jumped up and asked for a box of matches. Jennifer duly obliged and Jim asked her to turn off the lights. He then took one of the matches out of the box, stood up and bent over. I tensed, wondering what was next. Jim struck the match and thrust the lighted match between his legs.

35

There was a loud whoosh of gas and a smell of putrid fish that would knock you over. A blue flash, a foot long, lit up the room, consuming Jim's aerobic fart.

I let out a howl of astonishment and fell backwards off the sofa, dragging Susan with me. We ended up in a pile on the carpet, she on top, laughing out loud. We had just sorted ourselves out and were back on the sofa holding hands when a loud knock heralded the arrival of her ladyship. Her eyes swept the room, missing nothing. 'Please have some consideration for Sir Edwin; he has a busy day tomorrow. He's meeting a delegation of Kelpers and needs his sleep.' We all looked sheepish as she exited.

For the rest of the week that the *Shack* was in port, Susan and I met regularly in the evenings. There was no holding hands in the street, but there was no doubt in my mind, at least, that I was in love.

On Friday, the *Shack* headed south. We were all out on the stern waving goodbye for two and a half years to what passed for civilisation, but to a much smaller audience than when we had arrived less than a week earlier. I looked for Susan, but there was no sign of her.

We had sailed from the Falklands to South Georgia and thence to the Signy Island base in the South Orkneys, to pick up the Powell Island summer survey party, which I was to join. So we headed straight for Powell Island. That 30-mile journey took six days due to the pack ice, which we had to plough through. I was surprised two months later when we were picked up from Powell Island to find there were two letters addressed to me with an FI stamp on them. I opened the first. I had never had a love letter from anyone and here were two from Susan. She had poured her heart out. Such passion was mesmerising and I was taken aback. My heart felt fit to burst. I practically swooned and was floating on air all day. I put them in my diary

36

and every time I picked it up I felt the glow. It was a great feeling for a 22-year-old.

~~~

The near sinking of the RRS *Shackleton* upset everybody's plans for the summer. The *Shackleton* had dropped us late in the day to Powell Island and proceeded up the Lewthwaite Strait, which was full of floating iceberg bits. Late that evening they rammed an ice floe and tore a 16ft strip out of the side of the boat, which began to fill up with water. After several hours of pumping out the water they were losing the battle to keep afloat. Multiple times, two of the sailors went over the side with a length of canvas they plugged into the gap, thus preventing the total sinking of the ship. The SOS brought the whale-catching ship *Southern Harvester* to their rescue and she stood off until HMS *Protector* arrived the following day. The *Shackleton* was then towed back to South Georgia for repair.

I was taken on a tour of the British bases along the Peninsula by the *Protector* and I ended up in Stanley for Christmas. The first thing I did was make a beeline for Sadie in the office, to check out what had happened during my absence. I was met with a sad face. She told me that Susan had been carted off on that week's *Darwin* to Blighty. But that wasn't the worst news; she had become engaged to one of the naval officers on the HMS *Protector*, the Royal Navy's only ship in the South Atlantic, there to protect Britain's interests in the Antarctic. I grieved quietly. However, two new letters full of passion arrived from Susan, posted before she'd left for the UK. They helped during the trials and tribulations, the isolation of the long Antarctic winter, even though we were no more.

The Day of the Convergence 1957

The *Shackleton* had left Port Stanley a couple of days ago, and was heading south east towards the island of South Georgia on that November day appropriately named 'the Day of the Convergence', in my diary. The closeness of Antarctica ran like a current around the ship. We started to feel wisps of colder air eddying around the fo'c'sle, where a knot of expedition members dressed in their JEOs (junior explorer's outfits) huddled, duffle-hoods pulled tight against the gradually thickening mist. The sea had grown calm and all one could hear or feel was the disembodied thumping of the engines echoing off the fleecy, ephemeral fog that came and went, leaving a sudden brightness and clarity.

'Right,' I said to John, 'time for the next one.' John was one of the medics on board who was heading for a southerly base on the Peninsula. He had 'volunteered' to help me find the Convergence, after a little arm-twisting. We both clattered across the dewy fo'c'sle, awash with fog, and galloped down the companionway to the waist. John grabbed the weighted line attached to the small tin flask, and with a 'Watch your head!' whirled it gaucho style (we had all been deeply impressed with the horsemanship of the Uruguayan gauchos while we were laid up in Montevideo waiting for an engine spare part) and slung it forward, dropping it neatly ten yards off, running the line through his gloved fingers. Within seconds, the haul-in began. By that time, I had hauled alongside the line with the thermometer, and with a few quick hand-over-hands was writing the temperature.

Not only were we tracing the surface temperature changes that would indicate reasonably closely when we were across the Convergence, but we were hunting for a tiny animal, a member of that floating mass of sea life called plankton. Once we were across the 'line', this minute shrimp-like form, *Euphausia frigida*, would appear. It is not found on the north side, nor are its two cousins, *E. vallentini* and *E. longirostris* ('he of the long nose') found south of the demarcation zone.

Feeling the time had come (as well as the fact that I was running out of volunteers), I shot below to squirt a drop of the sample onto a glass microscope slide, slid it onto the stage of the binocular microscope, and hurriedly searched the field to see if 'long nose' was still present. If it was, I could dispense with trying to decide if the new life forms twitching and jerking in the glare of the microscope's light were *frigida* or not.

No long noses! Great! I called out to John. 'No need to stand around in wet drawers any longer; we're in the Antarctic! I'll buy you a beer on the strength of that.'

John, overcome by my generosity, paused – he, after all, was a Scot. 'I'll not drink that refrigerated urine,' he exclaimed.

'Sure, I suppose it's that bloody Scottish weak tea that passes for whiskey you'll be wanting,' I replied, laying on the ould-sod-type accent thickly.

'It's no wonder that Scots are a race of quivering eejits still suffering under the Sassenach yoke,' I continued, harking back to two old themes, which, though much hacked about, taken together were always sure to get a rise, like a golden minnow does when floated over a clear pool in the upper reaches of the River Blackwater in Co. Waterford. John paused in the cabin's doorway, turning deliberately back, hackles rising. Before the blasphemous utterance could be made, I hastily got in with 'I'll make it a double.' He grinned and said, 'Come on away.'

Having diverted the storm, I couldn't resist the final crack. 'Anyway, we'll beat shit out of ye in Murrayfield.'

We stared out at the fast unravelling knot on the fo'c'sle, heading head down for the bar. 'I hear we're there?' said Jim enquiringly from the doorway.

'Yes, our resident bogman found his frigid member of the plankton,' replied Alan knowledgeably.

'If we'd stayed out there any longer,' added John, carefully wiping the whiskey off his stubble and licking his finger, 'we'd have found our own digits rigid.'

'I'll drink to that!' came from the corner.

An air of contentment filled the lounge. We had passed another milestone on our 8,000-mile journey. Antarctica did exist. In fact, it was outside the door, and we were well on our way to realising our dreams.

~~~

In late November 1957 the *Shack* pulled into Signy Island, one of the smallest islands in the South Orkney group, much delayed by the ancient pack ice surrounding it. Then started the frantic effort to unload a year's supply of food and, most importantly, coal to keep all fires burning. Humping fifty-pound coal sacks was my first job in the Antarctic. Coal provided the only form of heating in the base hut and had to be used sparingly. One way of saving it was by not lighting the fire in the communal dormitory unless the temperature fell below freezing: 32°F. The coal moving exhausted me, so I crept into the base hut and sneaked up into the loft. There I found a pile of old and worn-out sleeping bags and curled up, fully clothed. I was instantly asleep.

I'd thought that Signy Island was to be my permanent base for the next two and a half years, but I discovered I was leaving the next day to travel to Powell Island to join the survey party who were going to map the island. The following morning I was shocked awake by the ship's whistle announcing that she was leaving – without me! I dashed down, emerging from the base hut, and ran down the jetty to the scow tied up, but only just, with the impatient third officer scowling at me. 'Where the hell have you been?' he barked as I jumped in. Instantly he untied the scow and we were off.

It took us nearly a week to get to Powell Island due to the heavy pack ice that the *Shack* had to plough through. She finally dropped us off but, two and a half hours later, she hit an ice floe and started to sink. Only for heroic efforts by two sailors who volunteered to go over the side into the freezing Antarctic waters, multiple times, to stick a patch on the sixteen-foot-long tear in the hull, the ship would have gone down. The banner headline in the *Sunday Independent* in Ireland that weekend read 'Irishman in Antarctic Drama' and I wasn't even on board!

We were on Powell to do a topographical survey of the island. Although its outline and coastline had been mapped for navigation purposes, a proper survey of the interior was needed. The Argentines on the neighbouring Island of Laurie, only ten miles away, hadn't done it and they had been occupying their base there since 1904, having taken it over from Robert Bruce's Scottish Antarctic expedition when the UK refused to do so. Now, fifty-three years later, Britain was going to map the island. I was just the hanger-on. I was to do a seal survey and, in particular, study the Fur seals that were thought to inhabit Powell and the neighbouring islands. Quite how we were going to do that I didn't know, as we only had a 14ft clinker-built pram with a 2.5 h.p. Seagull outboard engine, and the Scotia Sea was, and is, one of the most storm-ridden seas in the world.

I hardly knew what the nearly extinct Antarctic Fur seal looked like. The only live seals I'd ever seen were in Dublin Zoo: as students, we'd had a field trip once a year to acquaint ourselves with the wildlife that didn't live in

Ireland. But the zoo had only two species of seals – common and grey. Fur seals were not part of the menagerie of zoological gardens around the world because they had been hunted to near extinction in the nineteenth century for their valuable and beautiful warm pelts.

Everything south of 60° latitude and south of the polar front was considered to be in Antarctica, as was anything south of the Antarctic Convergence, where seriously cold sea-water currents coming up from the Antarctic continent met the not-so-cold sub-Antarctic current. So these were practically my first steps on this hallowed land: the land consecrated by Scott and Shackleton, by Amundsen and Mawson, and Brown and Byrd, the people who opened up the Antarctic with their expeditions – men who were heroes to most.

It was love at first sight: my very first live Antarctic seals. They rotated their hind flippers forward so they could do a fair gallop balancing on their two front flippers. I learnt quickly that you didn't challenge the big bulls that were holding a piece of the beach as their territory. They would chase you, and my schoolboy sprinting prowess was put to the test several times that first day on the beach.

But here I was, standing not two yards from a somnolent seal snoozing away on the pebble beach just down from where we had landed from the RRS *Shackleton*, on the southern end of Powell Island. I think I was floating, at least my feet were hardly touching the ground, as I had crept up on this spotty-coated seal, which I presumed was a pup, without causing it to flicker its long eyelashes. After some practice, I could lie down beside them and stick a thermometer into all sorts of places without causing a stir. I could approach any animal, any bird, any living thing. I could sidle up and touch them without, in most cases, causing anything other than a somewhat startled look, a moment of appraisal and a return to slumber.

It was how you approached that mattered. Did you arrive six feet tall and tower over them, casting a threatening shadow? No, if you got down to their eye level and approached gingerly, crawling even, if they followed all of your movements, if no threat was perceived, then peace continued to reign.

Most of the threats for them came in the sea – Killer whales, Leopard seals and maybe other seals. Of course, if you were injured and lying on land, or in the sea for that matter, the scavengers, chief among them being the 'Stinkers' (Giant Petrels) would descend in a cloud to finish you off. And that prettiest of southern seabirds, the Cape Pigeon – decked out in white and dark-brown flecks all over, with bright, inquisitive black eyes – could scavenge with the best of them.

But this was my very first contact with wildlife living in a savage wilderness. I stood over the sleeping seal. Not a stir. Was it alive? It wasn't breathing, mouth and nostrils shut tight. I looked hard at its chest. After what seemed a long time, I saw a faint lift. Then, moments later, a rush of hot air from the opening nostrils, which condensed in the cold evening air – it was very warm according to my companions, at 6°F below (-2.4°C). Here was a sleeping seal. Do seals have to come out on land to sleep? Surely not. They have to migrate or disperse, so they spend long periods at sea. So, was this just R&R for this small seal?

Now that I knew it was alive, I got out my notebook and quickly sketched it. I did a heel-to-toe shuffle alongside; it was up to four feet long including the hind flippers. Less the flippers, it was just over two and a half feet, nose to tail. Its grey coat was speckled with white spots on the back, with fewer on the flanks.

I looked at my first truly Antarctic seal in an Antarctic setting with wonder and my first feeling of belonging. I was here, on a windswept, snow-covered island in the Antarctic, standing closer than I had ever been to a truly wild animal, so close I could reach out and touch it. The wonder grew: this was the life. I squatted down beside the roly-poly figure. It was so fat that it looked like a fur-covered British banger, that essential part of the standard diet on FIDS ships.

I slipped my hands out of my mitts, reached out and very gently touched its fur. It felt soft and sleek, oily even, no doubt to provide an extra layer of insulation which, together with the layer of blubber under the skin, would prevent it freezing on the frozen land and getting hypothermia in the sea. It was lying on its side, facing away from me. I gently stroked its side a couple of times and felt a twitch. The upper eye flickered open, the nose lifted up and it looked at me over the top of its head.

Instant panic! Grunts followed by a chattering of its jaws, clicking and clashing of teeth and a rumbling warble deep in its throat. A muscular ripple ran from head to toe. It rolled onto its front and was off at a gallop. Well, not quite a gallop. Its mother's milk is so rich in fat that it triples its weight in the first three weeks so its front flippers can't reach the ground and it can only move by undulating forward, plonking its chest on the ice-hard snow and pushing with its pelvis. It headed for the sea, only twenty yards away. I burst out laughing at its efforts to rush, provoked by my shuffle to keep up.

After some five or six undulations it paused, head down, puffed out. After a few seconds it was off again. Damn! I had forgotten to get the sex. Next time I would remember to look. It seemed to be minutes before it arrived at the edge, but was probably not more than one. It paused, looked at me sideways with its head cocked to give it binocular vision. Seeing that I wasn't following, it took a longer pause, no doubt to catch its breath for the

45

submerging ahead. It shuffled, head down, into the shallows. Once afloat, it tilted its head up to take a long look back at me, showing no sign of fear.

Then, without a ripple, it disappeared into the dark-blue depths.

I, too, paused. The smile lingered. I'd had a unique experience. Almost everywhere else, seals were being hunted by fishermen and so the seals' collective memory of conflicts over the millennia was imprinted on their psyche. Instinctively, the flight reaction kicked in, and the animal disappeared as fast as it could. Here, I was in a different world; one of peace and tranquillity, or so I believed. You could approach any species and they would show no fear unless you were aggressive. This is what the rest of the world should be about. But even I knew that that was just wishful thinking.

I stared at the waves. No sign of the seal. I had ruined its evening nap. Better head for camp and learn the lesson. We are only guests in this world, and I should do what my mother always told me to do if I was a guest in someone's house – behave.

~~~

I was finally dropped in Port Stanley in January 1958 and given a free hand to fly around the two main islands of the Falklands and to see if I could find Fur seals, which I did. But with a relatively small number of Fur seals scattered around the coasts, no one was interested in starting a Fur seal industry in the Falklands, least of all the governor, Sir Edwin. Finally the powers-that-be decided that I should go back to Montevideo and report on the Uruguayan fur-seal industry, which was located on a single island – Isla de Lobos. I should work for the winter (which down there is June, July and August) with Professor Raul Vaz Ferreira, who I had met on the way south. By the time that was arranged, HMS *Protector* was heading home and, as she was paying an official visit to Montevideo, I would go with her.

The *Protector* had an extensive social programme in Monte with invitations streaming in for every hour of the day and night – one was for breakfast at 8.30, designed, I believe, to catch the young officers returning from the hectic night life. I went to every party and by the time it came for us to depart and leave me in the hands of Mrs Hawkins, the English landlady out in Pocitos, I had met everyone in the British community.

I now had to settle in to work at the University's Laboratory of Vertebrate Zoology. When we first met, Professor Ferreira, who ran the laboratory, insisted I understand that all the work going on in Uruguay on Fur seals was, if not secret, private, and I wasn't to collect the data or write reports without his express approval. He was intent on writing the definitive monograph on the species and he didn't want me feeding data to someone who might beat him to the punch, as it were. Having said that once, it was never mentioned again and there was no restriction on seeing the raw data or otherwise accessing the unpublished information lying around.

Though Raul subsequently produced a number of interesting scientific papers on the breeding ecology of *Arctocephalus australis*, the South American (and Falklands) Fur seal, his monograph never saw the light of day. He died in 1992. I've always hoped that all the work carried out over twenty-five years might someday throw light on those wonderful animals in a wonderful location.

Every time I look at a map and see Punta del Este printed on the headland that marks the real end of the influence the River Plate estuary on the Uruguayan coast, I think of my time there at HMG's expense. Soon after my arrival, Raul said we should take a preliminary trip to Isla de Lobos – appropriately 'the island of seals' – which lies about 8 km off Punta (as everyone in Uruguay calls it). He would also bring some rat-sized break-back traps to see if we couldn't catch a few rodents or their relatives in the hinterland of Maldonado, which is where Punta is located.

Not only is Uruguay's capital on the sea, but in twenty minutes you can walk from Plaza Artigas in the heart of the city to the beach. From there the beaches stretch to the Brazilian border, cove after cove after cove: Pocitos, Carrasco, Solis and then in a straight line miles long to the north, until you arrive at the still pristine beaches on both sides of the headland of Punta where the resort lies. The contrast of the affluence of Punta and the barren island lying offshore was considerable.

Isla de Lobos is about a kilometre long by half a kilometre wide. It's quite low – probably not more than 200 metres high – and has gently sloping sides and a flat top, which has been divided in part into paddocks to facilitate the handling of the Fur seals during the killing season. We 'camped' in the sealer shed, for me warm and snug after being down south, for Raul cold and damp after his central heating in Pocitos. I was brought around the paddocks where the seals were driven up from the coast (a mere 200 yards) to be funnelled into different pens depending on whether they were for the chop or not. The intention was to take only subadult males but, like all these operations, once the observers departed for coffee anything went, and there was no independent inspection of the kill. Despite the obvious laxity in regulating the industry, the population was (apparently) being maintained at a satisfactory level. In other words, the annual take of immature males was more or less constant. However, once I got to know the score I had a strong impression that the figures were being manipulated to keep the industry in business. Eventually this or market forces, or a combination of both, caught up with them, and the industry went into decline and closed down in the seventies. Efforts to revive it surface regularly but currently none exist. Once the workers skilled at skinning and treating the pelts departed, it was virtually impossible to carry on without investing in mechanisation and the development of technology to deal with a depleted workforce.

Having inspected the killing grounds that first evening, I walked down to the sloping rocks that the seals seemed to prefer – perhaps it was the reflected heat – and sat down in the evening sun not twenty-five yards away from a group of mothers and pups. Most of the adults were draped over a rock or lying on their backs in a crevice, waving their long fore or hind flippers in the air. The flippers fore and aft are practically devoid of fur, and waving them in the air allows the blood vessels close to the surface to be cooled. Having a double coat of outer and under fur in a climate like Uruguay's is a real problem for the seals, and lying out of the water on hot rocks in temperatures of 40°C in the sun means that overheating is a problem. The young pups, whose thermoregulation mechanism only comes into operation ten days or so after birth, tend to lie in the mother's shadow, getting a dual benefit of shade and closeness to a ready supply of rich milk – to say nothing of the protection needed in an active rookery, where frustrated harem masters regularly pick up pups and sling them around, even lashing them repeatedly off the rocks with, as you can imagine, fatal results.

I was greeted by a collection of raised heads and a few barks from some of the females, others merely glancing up and ignoring me. Among the weaned and un-weaned pups there was an initial scatter, but once you made no moves and sat stoically in the same place, normality returned. The pups were crowding into a rock pool, their black coats glistening wet, their eyes constantly flashing from friend to foe, all the while watching out for the menacing approach of the harem master, or perhaps even worse of his arch-rival, who needs to work off his aggression on those who can't bite back.

After 36 hours on the Island we left Punta on a gloriously sunny afternoon and survived the drive up the coast in Raul's ancient Studebaker. Driving in Uruguay, I'm told, is better than elsewhere in Latin America – and I'm still alive to prove it. But we did nearly have a crash. At one point there was a lull in the conversation. Raul's English was excellent; he had done his postgrad in North America and spent long periods in the Natural History Museum in London, researching the history of the fauna of Latin America from Darwin onwards, having already tackled the archives in the Museo Nacional de Ciencias Naturales on Paseo de la Castellana in the heart of Madrid's embassy row.

So when I spluttered 'Look! Look!' he looked around hastily while jamming on the brakes, shouting 'What? What? What?' Fortunately no one in the line of cars behind was dozing – it was eleven in the morning – and all swerved adroitly at approximately 60 mph, leaving the Studebaker shuddering to a halt. I stared out the window, pointing. Raul, puzzled again, said, 'What?' 'Oranges on trees,' I replied. He looked at me in astonishment. Before he could ask the question, I gave him the answer. 'Never saw that before – oranges come in boxes in Ireland.'

He started to laugh; deep inside, the reverberations shook his frame. The Studebaker rocked on its ancient springs. Tears streamed down his face. I grinned inanely. Every time he looked at me another paroxysm of laughter shook his not inconsiderable frame. Finally, exhausted, he lay back on the headrest, pulled out a hankie and wiped his face. He turned and smiled. 'I haven't had such a laugh in a long time. I will, how to say in English, dine off this for a long time.' Subsequently, every time I was introduced in Spanish to a new colleague the story was repeated.

But Isla de Lobos was just the start of the excitement. After a night on the island we moved back to more salubrious surroundings in Punta and the following day drove out three or four kilometres into the hinterland of the province of Maldonado, to see if we could catch some rodent-sized mammals. Running a trap line was something I knew how to do, but where in such an environment do you put the trap? Do you put them up trees (there's plenty of arboreal rodents)? In burrows – but might you just catch those beautiful big-eyed burrowing owls who measure three or four inches on their tippy-toes? Raul smiled at my questions. 'Let me,' he said, walking off into the bush. I did my bit by carrying the sack filled with break-back traps, so called because that's what they do.

Raul dropped some sort of smelly oil into the traps' tray and tucked them in the most unlikely places, or so it seemed to me. Once all were out and set, we reported to the local bistro for a well-earned meal.

The following morning, before breakfast, we were off to the hinterlands once again. Plastic trays at the ready, we prowled the trap lines. Mostly nothing: a few *Rattus rattus*, the black rat of bubonic-plague fame. You recognise them by the length of their tail, which is longer than the head and body together. Don't be fooled by the name: some black rats are quite dark, but many are all shades of brown.

After wading through the semi-bush for what felt like hours – it was already steamy hot at 8.30 am, with only two traps to go – an exclamation from Raul stopped me in my tracks. 'Ah,' he said. 'What?' I said. 'Wait till you see this,' he said, holding up the trap with a twig. Crushed in the middle by the heavy spring-loaded bar was what looked like a slightly chubbier rodent with a sort of variegated coat. 'Ah,' repeated Raul. 'I've wanted to catch one of these for ages.' 'What is it?' I asked again. He looked down his nose at me, his double chin quivering. 'It's a spiny rat, in fact the only one in this part of the world. You know what, the last person to catch one of these here was Charles Darwin – during the voyage of the *Beagle*,' he exclaimed triumphantly. I stretched my hand out to touch the body of the species that Darwin had touched. A strange exhilaration spread through me. '*Que plata*,' as they say in Montevideo. 'What a plate!' meaning 'What a surprise!'

However, even at that age I was developing a strong cynical urge. 'How do you know Darwin caught this particular species in this particular place?' Raul smiled knowingly. 'Because I've seen the original specimen in the Natural History Museum in Cromwell Road – the one that the original species description comes from.' 'Oh,' I said, 'but how do you know nobody has collected them since?' 'I checked,' he said. 'The Peabody Museum Expedition to Latin America in 1912. I'll write to the director of the Natural History Museum telling him we now have the second specimen in captivity.' He chuckled quietly, thinking of the stir in the Mammal Room in Cromwell Road when his letter arrived.

We departed for Monte feeling content. I had seen the seals close up and touched the flesh that touched Darwin's. A great couple of days and a great start to my stay. Raul said to all on our return that I brought him luck; we did quite a lot of trapping together afterwards, but nothing came up to that height of achievement.

~~~

The story has a sequel. Later, after my sojourn writing up the results of all those labours for FIDS at Charing Cross Hospital Medical School, I moved to University College Cork as a very junior lecturer. (UCC was originally Queen's College Cork, set up in 1849 by Queen Victoria at the same time as Queen's College Belfast, which never felt the need to change its name, except to upgrade itself to a university – such notions.) UCC had had a superb

52

zoological museum, housed in Victorian glass cases in a specially built gallery in the main building. By the time I got there, the collection was suffering the ravages of neglect and the pressures of the university developers who regarded stuffed animals as much less worthy than stuffing knowledge into living students. So the collection had been gradually eroded, or dispersed to whoever would take it. But the museum was a mine of objects that could illustrate classes, both practical and theory, and I paid quite a few visits to hunt among the mouldering dust-shrouded remains for likely specimens.

One morning, while doing a search, I picked up a mouldy stuffed marsupial. The name was so dirty and faded that 'marsupial' was all I could easily make out. The words after looked like *Smith Aeria*. I turned over the wooden board to which it was pinned. Some faint writing – I wet a finger and rubbed away the dust and dirt – faintly, a nine-letter word gradually appeared with repeated rubbing: *Maldonado*. I rushed off and got a sponge and some detergent. As I cleaned off the century of dirt and grime a line appeared: 'Collected by C. Darwin' and a reference no. My heart leapt. This was a real specimen collected by the naturalist of the *Beagle* and given to the Natural History Museum. How had it arrived in Cork?

I immediately rang Gordon Corbett, the Director of Mammals in Cromwell Road and an old mate of mine. I told him the story, and he said, being a canny Scot, he'd come back to me. A few days later a phone call assured me that it was a genuine specimen collected by Darwin. Apparently in the setting up of the Queen's colleges, the British Museum was asked to contribute unneeded specimens to start off their museum collections, and some of Darwin's and others went missing. (I subsequently found one from

Malaysia collected by Sir Stamford Raffles, which was part of the same handout.)

Naturally, Dr Corbett politely – in fact very politely – asked for the return of the Darwin specimen. You can imagine the reply.

~~~

I arrived back in Montevideo in April 1958 on HMS *Protector*. Working with Raul on the Fur seals of Uruguay was exciting. The amount of seals en masse was a new experience for me. My life there revolved around Mrs Hawkins' boarding house in Pocitos, the university down near the port, and the cricket club in Carrasco.

While most of the passing bods in the boarding house spoke English, the university was different. Though most of the senior academic staff spoke English, few wished to, so that unless technical explanations became impossible I tried, without much success, to take it all in Spanish. Still, the nuts and bolts of population dynamics and reproductive physiology of South American Fur seals is the same in Spanish as in English, and I muddled through. Despite the linguistic and cultural differences, it was really exciting to be able to get to grips with the genus *Arctocephalus*, which included all the species of Fur seals whose life I had headed south to explore.

Having seen only one southern Fur seal on Powell Island, and that one dead, I started off thinking that the ecology and behaviour of this population would be very close, if not identical, to those inside the Antarctic Convergence. Yet very early on I was having doubts. Once I had spent some days sitting cheek to jowl with the breeding harems, I began to suspect that the males at least were quite different. Yet when I got to Bird Island in South Georgia, I immediately had no doubt that we were dealing with a different race or species. However, interest in Fur seal society was intense in scientific circles, and I should not have been surprised that permission to collect (the polite word for shoot) a few adult males and transport their skulls to Cromwell Road for the attention of Judith King was turned down in South Georgia on the basis that it might affect the stability of the emerging population on Bird Island, which was growing at least 7-10 per cent per annum. Nigel Bonner, the Elephant seal inspector, was studying this population, having set foot on Bird Island at least once, and would in due course supply the museum with the specimens necessary to make an evaluation. In other words, forget it.

This was 1958, long before studies of DNA, genes and genomes, and the only way to distinguish between species or subspecies or races was to measure their bodies, but more importantly their skulls, in some detail to distinguish consistent differences. If those were obvious enough, one might as a result describe a new species. That of course was the prize. It's a form of scientific immortality: one's name appears in the scientific literature forever as the discoverer of this or that new species.

Of course if you do it for insects, finding names for the hundreds of new ones that are discovered every year, even today, is a struggle. But a new mammal? That's an order of magnitude or two better. There are only 6,495 mammal species so far recognised in the world, as against 30 million-plus insect species. Potentially there are a few million hiding in the remnants of tropical forest still left standing. Standing, that is, until the ranchers, gold or mineral miners, oil prospectors and tourism operators get them, which will extinguish them even before climate changes them irrevocably.

Climate change was then unknown, but the work then being carried out in Antarctica internationally by fourteen countries during the IGY was going to change all that. My friend Joe Farman, who would end up in Halley Bay at the head of the Weddell Sea, had the year before headed for Stonington Island and would ultimately head up the team that would astrophysically turn the planet on its head and reveal the ozone hole that was growing like a halo above Antarctica. Joe had gone down south to confirm or refute the theory that the Earth's surface crust was made up of a jigsaw of plates that floated around over geological time, bumping into each other, causing mountains to form where they collided; or deep rifts (the Great Rift Valley is one example) where they dived under one another.

The Wegener theory of plate tectonics had been around since 1912 but had largely been derided and ignored. Joe's observations on the magnetism of Antarctic rocks, along with the network of other observations around the continent during IGY (which to confuse everyone, was eighteen months and not twelve), proved Wegener right and changed our perception and understanding of the world for ever.

Joe's subsequent work on the physics of the upper atmosphere led to the gradual dawning that man's machinations had the potential to annihilate humanity. Is there a point at which the saturation of the atmosphere with chemicals spewed out by billions of cars, cookers, fridges, factories, cows, etc. will, without giving our leaders/politicians the chance to decide otherwise, cross the threshold after which all there is a collapsing system, which, within a decade or two (or three) – too short for any political response – will bring devastation, anarchy and despair to all the planet, so that even the affluent will not survive? Is this just far-fetched? Is there any evidence that this has happened in the past? The short answer has to be no. But probably at no time since the emergence of man as the dominant force on this earth have we been more intent on destroying the natural world. For what?

Money, of course.

Interlude

After a disastrous start to my first Antarctic season, what with the *Shackleton* plunging into an iceberg, having just deposited us on Powell Island, HMS *Protector* came to the rescue and nursed the *Shackleton* to South Georgia for necessary repairs. *Protector* then set out to complete her other priority duties before remembering that we – the Powell Island Summer Party Expedition – should also be rescued. Of course no one told us: our radio schedules with the base at Signy were poor to non-existent; too many mountains in the way, Cecil said with a smile. With my binoculars I could see Signy Island across a beautiful stretch of the Scotia Sea. So, one sunny afternoon, just weeks into our sojourn, who came down the strait between Coronation and Powell islands but the bold *Protector*, here to save these benighted explorers. We were supposed to be there for the rest of the summer but with the *Shackleton* out of action they needed to get us as soon as possible so we were not stranded.

A Morse lamp blurred out a message. Desperately we, alerted by Scotty who had been having a quiet kip on a sunny moss bank, racked our brains for the remains of the Morse code last used to win a scout badge. 'I think they want us to come up on some channel or other,' I guessed. 'What's the emergency channel?' Cecil asked. '116,' came the reply. A rush to get out the radio set, which weighed about 15–20 lbs, and generator and crank it up to speed.

After much fecking around, a voice boomed, '*Protector* to Powell Island party – the skipper would like a word.' The stentorious voice hoped we were all fit and well and said that the Royal Navy was here to help us out of our little difficulty, and we would be embarked *tout de suite*. A pinnace (a sort of a motor boat) was duly put over the side and on it, a minion, who, glancing at our shambles of a base camp as he arrived on shore, asked, 'Can we help, old chap?'

But I wasn't going anywhere. My programme had only just begun. As the basic geographical survey of the island was now done, everyone had agreed that the next push would be on the Fur seals. We were all geared up to cross the ice-strewn strait between Powell and Ellefsen Island, our nearest neighbour. It looked formidable: a sharp-toothed jaw of an island with impossible steep slopes and, as far as I could see with binoculars and telescope, a few tiny rock-strewn beaches.

So the arrival of *Protector* with a demand to leave was not to my liking. I took Cecil aside. If they wanted to take me around Ellefsen that would be fine, but we had another six weeks' work here. Cecil smiled, and said 'Why don't you tell him?' 'Yes, I bloody well will!' Jutting my jaw and clenching my teeth, I strode down to the pinnace. I stared the subbie straight in the eye. 'I have a message for your skipper: we're not leaving!' He looked somewhat astonished. 'Come with me,' he replied.

I jumped aboard and followed him into the cabin. He picked up the radio phone and said, 'Chief, this is subbie in the pinnace. We seem to have a problem: we have some ...' he paused and looked at me – 'some scientific lad who says they can't leave, something to do with Fur seals and such.' 'You what? Get that spotted dick and I'll sort him out!' bellowed forth from the phone. 'I have him here, Sir' – hastily handing me the phone. 'Chief, this is Fergus O'Gorman. I'm the scientist you were referring to.' I paused for breath: it's not often a 22-year-old takes on the first officer of a bloody great warship.

Before I could continue, the chief responded with much more dolce tone. 'We have a really tight schedule to keep which has been put out of kilter by this very necessary no doubt side trip. We appreciate your concern for science and all that but we're here to help see that no untoward things happen and if they do to sort them out. I have an ETD of 1700 hours when we will leave. I have a contingent of twenty Royal Marines on board. If you insist I will send them to help you pack up. Would that be a help?'

Three months' equipment, food and camping gear, to say nothing of all my scientific specimens and stuff, are not easily packed and dispatched in a couple of hours, but we did get away at 1900. We steamed at full throttle to Signy and dropped Cecil and the lads plus all the gear at the double, or, as the Chief said to me as we steamed away, 'That was done two-six' (at maximum speed). This was my first introduction to the Royal Navy way of doing things. In the next couple of years we were to have some interesting encounters together.

In between Powell and Signy I discovered that 'fresh orders had been issued with regard to depositing of the Fur seal wallah', and that I was to proceed on the *Protector* to Montevideo to work again with Professor Raul Vaz Ferreira in the university. This would avoid wasting six months of Antarctic wintering and I could get first-hand knowledge of the local Fur seals.

So now I had another panic. All my personal effects and gear were on Signy. I was going to have to pack whatever I needed for the next six months in about five minutes flat. I rushed ashore, looked for my gear still unpacked in the lab, and grabbed what I thought would be necessary for a sojourn in the Mediterranean climate of Montevideo. Another new horizon was opening up, just as the challenge of my first Antarctic summer faded into the background.

~~~

In the end, my five months in Montevideo were hectic. Work in the university during the day, play until late at night, training and playing rugby for the cricket club – at least until an opposing full-back broke my jaw in three places with a head butt! That slowed me down a bit until I had to head for Buenos Aires to join the Polish sealing crew heading for South Georgia and the Elephant seal kill.

Seeing South Georgia appear over the horizon made me feel like I suspect Ernest Shackleton did when he and four others made their astonishing journey in an open lifeboat from Elephant Island, 800 miles further south: the ice-covered cliffs and soaring peaks springing straight out of the sea made my heart miss a beat; it is really something to see mountains, snow-covered and glistening, go straight up to over 9,000 feet! It's as if you cut Everest and its neighbours Lhotse and Nuptse off at 19,000 feet and dumped them in the sea – truly a remarkable sight. Throughout the Antarctic Peninsula this chain of peaks appear, as the tips of the sunken chain of the Andes, stretching from Patagonia via South Georgia to the South Sandwich Islands and on to the islands of the South Orkneys and South Shetlands. They reappear as part of the Antarctic continent as the Antarctic Peninsula before heading for the Polar Plateau and becoming the Transantarctic Mountains at a height of 16,050 feet at Mount Vinson.

Arriving at the entrance to the haven of the fjord at Grytviken was such a relief after days of pounding by the South Atlantic. Here the sea appeared mirror calm (only six to nineteen feet waves). To stand on land was rocky but bliss. A punt was pulled up to the jetty awaiting my pleasure; I didn't even have to lug my overstuffed suitcase and rucksack the mile or so around Discovery Cove to Discovery Point, where HMG had her HQ and living quarters for visiting 'tourists'.

Grytviken was the first whaling station I had visited. We had landed at the main jetty within smelling distance of 'the Plan', the 250 square yards of decking on which the whales were drawn up and quartered. The foul smell was all-pervasive, and nowhere on this island could you get away from the only reason people were here – money. Most of the whalers were Norwegians from Sandefjord or Stavanger who, in a good season, could return home and not have to work for the summer, returning to South Georgia six months later for another bout of carnage.

I was determined to throw myself into my work and on my first morning rushed around to the whaling station to see when the first sealer would go to sea, only to discover that the season didn't start for another week. So I had an excuse, between report reading, to explore the island on foot.

Without access to a boat, climbing around the Grytviken fjord was the only way to get around.

However, on my second day out, coming back from summiting the local mountain, I had my first katabatic experience. And South Georgia, as I was to learn, was famous for them.

A katabatic bash is a huge wind off a glacier or snow cap which, rushing down to sea level, picks up enormous amounts of speed – it was so powerful that it simply flung me down the hill for about 20 ft. Fortunately I was walking on morainic mud, snow and gravel and the only result was scratched hands and face, torn knees, pain and shock. If I'd been further down in the high tussock grass, I could have broken my neck.

High up on the hill, I'd looked through binoculars at the huge cross on Discovery Point, put there by Shackleton's men after his death in Grytviken on 5 January 1922, and at the tiny cemetery that housed his remains along with those of many men, mostly Norwegian, who hadn't survived the isolation and dangers of South Georgia. Was Emily Shackleton right to send his body from Montevideo to Grytviken to return to the earth here, several thousand miles away from where he would have much preferred: somewhere close to the South Pole, or at least on the continent itself? Was it her realisation that if his body were returned to the UK, he would have been only one dead among many and seen as a failure? He had not only not crossed the continent as intended, but never got as far as setting a foot on it. Or was it that she couldn't bear the additional burden of sharing the graveside with Hope Paterson, who had supported Shackleton physically and financially for so long? Mythology prefers the first explanation, though his affair was well known.

I made it back to the camp to find the rest of the crew at the communal tea. As I stood there covered in a multitude of scratches and seal poo, to say nothing of the holes in my ex-army gear, someone asked what happened. 'I fell over,' I replied. Smiles all round. Did I see the katabatic display down the fjord, someone quipped. It must have gone on for at least ten to fifteen minutes. A slight grin flickered around the table, but no one laughed. Such was my introduction to this most glorious of sub-Antarctic islands.

Only a few weeks earlier, at the end of May 1958, the three men I'd shaken hands with at Signy the previous year, David Statham, Stanley Black and Geoffrey Stride, all died in the Dion Island disaster. They had taken a fully loaded sledge with a team of huskies out across the sea ice to Dion Island from the Horseshoe Island base, ostensibly as part of laying a depot for subsequent trips. But the real reason was to visit the newly discovered and only Emperor penguin rookery on the east coast of the Antarctic Peninsula. It was located on the sea ice. They camped on the sea ice but it broke up and the three men were lost, presumed drowned. Amazingly, the huskies survived, turning up at their base on Horseshoe Island, in one case almost six weeks later.

The following week I reported on the jetty for my first sealing voyage. Even though the tide was down, I expected the *Phoca* – a highly imaginative name for a sealer, the Spanish and Latin for 'seal' – to be alongside the half dozen whale catchers with their vicious grenade launchers sitting upright on the prow. But no, no sign unless the mast head just peering above the jetty had something connected to it? And there it was, all 90 tonnes and 55 feet of it. You mean that six sealers, the three crew and I were going out into the South Atlantic in that? For a moment I nearly balked, but as I was the only (temporary) sealing inspector in South Georgia the voyage couldn't go without me. I was standing in for the Sealing Inspector who was still in the UK as his wife was having a baby. After all, HMG needed to know how many seals were shot and how many delivered on the plan; this was all about money and control – it was, after all, British territory, as the Argentines were to find out to their cost in 1982.

I jumped down onto the deck, grinned a hello to the Poles I'd met on the trip from Buenos Aires, and shook hands with the tough-looking, gingery-blond Norwegian skipper. We'd be out for five or six days and should come back with maybe 500 Elephant seal skins. In the previous century all the beaches would have been packed with Fur seals, which had much more valuable pelts, most of which were salted and sold on the Asian market. They were decimated by the end of the nineteenth century, and it was as a result of a sealing exploration trip by Salvesen's from Sandefjord that the extent of the whale resource became obvious, leading to the whaling stations in Stromness and Grytviken being set up in 1904, with five others in the following years. After World War II the race to provide whale oil for margarine and products in the cosmetics industry meant that within twenty years the whale populations in the South Atlantic were commercially extinct.

During that 1958 season, the feeding frenzy was at its height. When we started out, the fjord was mirror-calm, reflecting the surrounding snow-covered hills. As we approached the mouth the boat started to feel the swell building up. The skipper muttered something about a bit of a swell and that we would be going north and not south as intended. The significance of this comment went straight over my head until we arrived at the mouth. At this point the tiny *Phoca* literally stood on its tail, the bow riding up on a huge swell and plunging down the other side. From one minute to the next the calm became endless ups and downs. I had never been seasick up to that moment. I had survived the Bay of Biscay in October, the roaring forties, the frightful fifteens and the howling sixties in the Drake Passage below Cape Horn, and never a drop regurgitated.

But in the instant *Phoca* climbed skywards I felt a rush like none before and hurriedly, encouraged by the skipper, shot out of the bridge to bring up my stomach-full of greasy rashers, sausages, eggs and toast. Before we reached the first trough I had provided several meals for the skein of Stinkers that had just joined us from the headlands and would swoop and stick with us to every beach and killing ground, where they would feed like vultures, bloody heads buried inside the abandoned seal carcasses.

Despite this continuous *mal de mer*, once we anchored in the bay in front of a beach crowded with female Elephant seals, often in groups of twenty or more, minded by a dominant bull, I had to go over the side into the enlarged Norwegian pram with the sealers, which they rushed through the breakers, crashing onto the beach. As we approached the beach at least two of the crew at the prow jumped over into the freezing water and held the head to prevent the punt from broaching.

Sometimes all six were over the side, leaving me and the outboard engine driver to hold our breaths. However, in all the days and weeks of sealing that I observed, never once did the dinghy broach to, though there were many close calls. We would rise at seven and never finished until dark: these men would go ashore maybe up to four to six times depending on the closeness of the beaches, and, having got there wet and cold, would set about the bloody business of removing all the bulls on that beach.

The Elephant seal social system made the hunt straightforward. Adult Elephant seals reach sexual maturity at five years of age but are not normally socially mature until they are nine years old. He defends his territory from other bulls or anything else that might appear threatening. He may weigh four tonnes (900 lbs), is twice if not four times the size of females and can rear up on his fore flippers to about eight or nine feet. When the male rushes up to you, bellowing and inflating his huge nostrils, he blasts his fetid breath all over you, loaded with the remnants of digested squid, krill and fish. The odour from his lower gut seems to be driven up to join the foamy sputum he generates with his inflamed nostrils. His bloodshot eyes, and the open bleeding wounds around his head and neck sustained in the field of battle, persuade you to turn and flee. He will pursue you at full tilt, but only for ten or twenty yards, so not to worry.

Killing one of these bulls was easier than shooting an apple off his head. Rarely did the crew leader – the one with the gun – have to get that close. Once you approached a group of somnolent cows with a bull lying among them, the bull would rear up and hold his ground as the females scattered. He could then be shot from ten or twelve feet. Normally two head shots finished him off, but on one memorable occasion I photographed a bull taking four rounds as he charged down the beach and plunged into the water, turning it blood red before disappearing. Even the hardened sealers shook their heads in amazement.

Once he's downed, another shot into the head may be necessary from close range if there is any sign of life. And then the bloody work begins. A slash through the carotid artery usually brought a spout of arterial blood gushing like a fountain to stain the snow for yards around. The flensing of the tough skin starts from the base of the skull, and goes down to the insertion of the hind flippers. Then the job of rolling this enormous carcass over using hand picks, with everyone, except me, tugging. Once the flensing is completed, the skin is pulled down and thrown into the surf where it floats, washing out more blood. While this is going on the shooting continues until every available male of any size is taken. The theory is that there are so many socially immature males hanging around that once we leave the beach all these young males will look after those demanding females.

The skins were then towed out to float behind *Phoca* on lines – with all that fat, they floated high in the water. Within minutes, hordes of Cape Pigeons, the lovely dark-brown and white Petrels, descended, picking off the blood and sucking down the fat globules. This screaming, heaving mass of bird bodies stayed together until we upped anchor and headed for the next beach and the next bloody encounter. And I went back to being sick.

While every trip to a beach gave me a couple of hours of respite, as the week progressed I became weaker. All I could do on the beach was record the kills and make sure no females were taken.

When I woke up in the morning a sup of water was all that I was taking, then onto the flying bridge to maintain the maximum fresh-air flow and be prepared for any other activity. Returning around the headland into the calm

68

of the fjord at Grytviken on a Friday evening was like entry to paradise. I had the weekend to recover. Monday we would be out again. So much for the holiday trip to South Georgia! Amazingly, this was my last bout of *mal de mer* in two and a half years in the Southern Ocean, or ever since for that matter.

Despite the bloodiness of the sealing business, for me the great adventure was that we went into virtually every bay and beach on South Georgia, a chance that few have had before or since. Every visit, every beach, every bay was new. Experiences piled onto experiences. Some memories still stand out, as fresh as if they had happened yesterday.

My first time in St Andrew's Bay to kill seals among the largest King penguin rookery on the island, perhaps in the world, was a delight. These birds stand – and they do really stand – at more than two feet and weigh 25 lbs. They are second only to the Emperor in that regard, and like the Emperor incubate their large single egg on their toes, keeping it warm with a large flap of abdominal fat and feathers, which hangs down over it. It's rather like a low-slung pregnancy, or rather a pompous male geriatric shuffling along with over-developed pot – for it's the males that, as with the Emperors, do most of the incubation.

A crowd of Kings paraded up the beach to where the vast majority of their young were now hatched and standing around waiting to be fed, wearing what for all the world looked like a fluffy brown bear-skin, but in reality was the body coat of down that later in the season they would shed for the glossy deep-blue feathers of their adult coat. Like all animals who have the benefit of living away from man's benevolence, these were amazingly tame, and with a cautious and careful approach you could sit among them and within moments your presence was ignored. Seeing wildlife close up in those days before universal TV was a revelation.

But though those days stand out as a privilege, it was another sight that really stayed in my memory. Among the greeting group of penguins there seemed to be a lot of dead young ones, all in their woolly coats. Many had died sometime before, maybe up to a week or ten days, and in the interval the snow had melted all over the beach except under their small prone bodies, so many ended up draped over a pillar of snow. It looked for all the world like a penguin cemetery.

Hanging out round the plan gave me something to do even though I had no official function beyond being a sealing inspector. I often watched the whales being delivered lying floating in a long row side by side, Sei beside Blue, Fin beside Minke, the big and the not so big. These were always left until last or until the whaling inspector went to lunch. Then there would be a sudden flurry and the undersized or the heavily pregnant would be rushed into the plan and dispatched with great speed to avoid any report of an illegal catch.

But hanging around had a benefit. I got talking to the Norwegian crews of the whale catchers and in due course got invited to go out for a couple of days when whales were reported close in to the island. My abiding memory is of the ones shot at with the explosive grenade but only wounded, with the harpoon flying loose and the clouds of blood as the whale dived (and died?) I can still hear the bang of the harpoon being fired and the dull thud as it exploded inside the whale. This was followed by a surge of blood and flesh erupting into the freezing air and condensing into a pink cloud above the gaping wound, while the four steel barbs released by the explosion slammed wide open, driving into the whale's lacerated muscle bed and gripping like the claw of some prehistoric flying pterosaur. Then there was the twenty-minute struggle of whale versus ship before, perhaps, a second shot could finish the job and silence the high-pitched screams issuing every time its head came above the water. But more likely it was banged in, the heavy springs on the two-inch-thick cable on the harpoon pulling it tight with the capstan in reverse, inexorably drawing the dying whale back to the surface where it lay exhausted, though rarely dead, to be finished off at leisure. It seemed obscene that while a whale lay panting alongside the catcher and pulsating gushes of blood poured forth from the man-sized wound in his thorax, a thick rubber hose was inserted into his abdomen and he (there were supposed to be no females) was pumped full of air, so that he could float with a radio beacon on top of a flagged pole to allow the towing vessel to find and retrieve that carcass along with any other killed that day.

When the dying whale finally surfaced, everyone on board let out a roar of triumph (except me, of course), and that evening alcohol was handed round and the toast was 'More whales, more money in the bank,' which brought forth huge smiles and a round of back-slapping. Needless to say, this would not happen today and, with the demise of the whaling industry in the mid-sixties and the near extinction of most of the whale species, public attitude changed. The environment movement – of which I was an active member – lobbied internationally for the protection of whales, and to our delight we succeeded.

~~~

That season two former Fids arrived in Grytviken to set up a three-year study of the Wandering Albatross on Bird Island, off the northern tip of the main island. Appropriately named, this island was alive with birds, having the largest Macaroni penguin rookery in the world – over a million birds – and a host of Albatross species: all in fact of those in that part of the Southern

71

Ocean. Lance Tickell, who had been base leader of Signy before Cecil Scotland, had while he was there, though not employed as a biologist, done the very first study of the Fairy Prion – a group of small Petrels that lived under the rocks at the cliff behind the base hut. He now wanted to tackle the Albatrosses, especially the greatest, the Wandering, whose wingspan measures up to twelve feet! Of course with that going for them, circumnavigating the Southern Ocean – a round trip of 23,000 miles (in a straight line) – comes easier than for most, but in those days we couldn't be sure. The ringing programme started to track the dispersion of the Giant Petrels from Signy, a programme that Dick Laws had begun in the early fifties, and was throwing up interesting clues. He was the first biologist employed by FIDS (I was the second).

In the days before satellites and radio tracking, the only way to follow bird migration or dispersion was by putting an aluminium ring on the bird's leg. Normally this was done at the nest site when the fledglings were large enough that the ring would not fall off, or when the leg had more or less reached adult size. As Giant Petrels' nests were a collection of stones on open hillsides, the young were easy to catch and ring. Most other Petrels nested in burrows or on cliffs, making a large-scale operation difficult or hazardous, as Roger Filer was to find to his cost. Before I left Signy, I had trained Roger how to ring the Petrels living at the rear of the base hut. He went on to do a study of the Paddies, and in the following year fell to his death from the cliffs at Gourlay while on a ringing expedition.

The preliminary work of Lance and others had started to show that some of these ringed birds died and were washed up on the beaches to the east of the Orkneys. Reports were coming in to the British Museum (whose address was printed on the ring) of landings first in South Africa, then Australia and

72

New Zealand, but none as yet from South America (birdwatchers in Patagonia were pretty thin on the ground). We were waiting for the first young to come back to Signy as adults, which they did in 1959. This was the first confirmation that these birds flew around and around the whole Southern Ocean for five years before appearing once again in the very place where they were born.

Lance and Pete Cordell, who accompanied him on that first Bird Island expedition, had a season with the Signy Stinkers and were anxious to start a similar study on the Albatrosses, not merely to confirm that they also disperse throughout the Southern Ocean but to discover the details of their biology in order to ensure their long-term conservation.

I went along for help and encouragement. But try as we might to land on Bird Island with a fierce north-easterly driving onto the only accessible beach, a reroute was required to the relative calm of the other side of the strait. The camp was set up and the season's work began, marking nest sites, trying out various techniques that allowed the catching of adults unharmed, ringing and collecting food samples. Initially, these were bits lying round the foot-high conical mounts into which the female Albatross deposited her single large egg. Later, methods of extracting the gut contents – without killing the bird – were devised. For me, these couple of days were a delight, away from the bloody routine of killing seals and doing something biologically useful with friends of a similar bent. Of course we discussed everything, except seal-killing!

I returned to Grytviken and to another month of sealing before the *John Biscoe* picked me up on its first voyage of the year, relieving the British bases. We called at Signy, where I was hoping to winter in 1959, but it took me to King George Island and to the Admiralty Bay base to pick up Alan

Sharman, and onto Deception where we picked up Pete Hodkinson, who was the third member of the Livingston Island Fur Seal Summer Party I was leading. The *John Biscoe* deposited us at its western end, for what turned out to be a couple of months of looking for Fur seals and only finding one female and her pup. However, that pup was the first recorded in that part of the Antarctic in nearly a hundred years, and was worth all the effort. Fame at last!

Snow and Space

Antarctica is a huge and essentially empty wilderness. Even at the height of the tourist season, in January and February, the maximum number of tourists landing on the continent and islands within the polar front hardly reaches 5,000. If you include the personnel of Antarctic bases, who nowadays are mostly summer visitors, you might double that number. Most of these would be in the US bases in McMurdo Sound and the South Pole. Nowhere, even in Siberia, are people thinner on the ground.

Not only is there space, but also the silence that goes with it. Soft snowflakes on a zephyr of wind float down without a sound. Fluffy, butterfly-size crystals descend to land in your hair, on your eyelashes, nose and cheeks with scarcely a whisper. Or maybe the whisper is imagined, a product of the instinctive blink to clear the vision, the flexing of cheeks, the puffing of breath up past one's nose to blow them back whence they came. But if you are perfectly still, hood up, hands in mitts, head tilted slightly up, ears pricked, mouth partly open, tasting the sound, you can hear it. In that infinity of space, it comes as a whisper from another world, one over which we have even less control – the atmosphere.

If I stayed statue still, I could sometimes hear the crystals popping on my skin with a sibilant hiss as they transformed from a solid stable state into water, using the energy supplied by my relatively glowing skin; relative, that is, to the sub-zero temperature of the snowflakes. Once they have melted, gravity takes over, silently pulling the new liquid droplet earthwards, its globular shape changing to linear, its surface area increasing exponentially, exposing it – despite its increased contact with my cheek – to the much lower temperature of the outside air. In an instant, it reverts to its previous state of

75

iciness, congealing into a tiny pebble of ice now firmly attached, frozen to my face.

In my junior explorer phase, I spent much time and effort trying to prevent such an accumulation, wiping my face regularly with a hankie. This worked for my face but left me quite quickly with a sodden and soon-to-be rigid piece of cotton in my anorak pouch. This then wet my field notebook, or even froze it. I soon abandoned that procedure and the hankie was kept for more important jobs, such as wiping condensation from the lenses of my camera or binoculars.

These were hung around my neck and generally tucked between my sweater and anorak or, depending on the air temperature, between my sweater and shirt. If I was sitting or standing outside my heat output would be low, and the waxes that lubricated the moving parts of both implements would congeal in the cold, making focusing impossible in the case of the binoculars. The camera shutter was similarly affected. Sometimes it wouldn't click at all.

Knowing which layer they should be kept under in order to function on demand was a matter of experience. I had to make the decision based on the air temperature, wind speed, and my activity level. In the direst conditions, that was next to the third layer, the string vest. I soon realised that putting a metal body close to mine may have guaranteed full lubrication for maybe thirty seconds, but most of those seconds would be spent clearing the lens of condensation or, if one fumbled around too much, trying to remove the skim of soft-focus ice that covered the lens in no time at all.

As my experience and my understanding of the variables grew, I let the snow and ice accumulate into a layer, invading and attaching to the roots of the outer perimeter of my beard. Once formed, this layer provided protection against further attack. Of course, there were occasions when the pustules formed such a patch that any attempt at their removal could cause more angst and pain than the frost-nip that might develop as a result of keeping them at bay.

The vision of snow etched into my cortex is not of large fluffy flakes, which were unusual, but of snow driven by the all-prevailing wind. Sharp slivers of snow crystals, driven nearly horizontal, stabbing one's cheeks, forcing an immediate attempt to cover up; pull the hood cord tighter, push the woollen scarf up to cover chin and, where possible, one's mouth. But that brought its own problems of condensing breath freezing to your beard. So it was always a compromise.

The only answer was to turn away from a direct confrontation with the wind unless your life depended on it, as so often it did. Cock your head to the side to take the onslaught on the side of the anorak hood, or just turn around and go back to the tent or the hut, and give up trying to do whatever it was you were trying to do, which in the larger scheme of things didn't matter a jot. It was always a toss-up to go or turn back. You didn't start in poor conditions of mist, fog or snow, but once you set out the imperative was to get to the other end, wherever it was, or suffer the snide comments of your fellow hut dwellers.

It wasn't just discomfort, or occasionally even pain, that falling snow or ice brought that mattered. What really mattered was the visibility. The landscape was over 95 per cent covered by snow and ice, and on the right day and in the right light, it was colourful and intensely beautiful. But most of the time it was whiter than white, with the surface features, when you could see them, merely a shade different, so that seeing cracks in the sea ice, or seal holes that were plugged with fresh snow, depended on the visibility at the time. In a few minutes, the landscape of icy hills and hummocks, already full of multiple pitfalls, could change and be obliterated by snow descending or being driven across the surface of the sea ice, the ice cap or off a glacier. To be caught out and unprepared for these sudden snow flurries was truly difficult and dangerous; you needed to have all your wits about you.

Drifting snow could, and did, vary through a wind range from mild to severe. Even on the best days, occasional flurries of snow of varying intensity would scurry across the surface, picked up by a breeze, which itself might be only five to ten miles an hour. This spindrift, dancing around my feet during my junior explorer phase, would cause me to raise my head and turn it, eyes widening and ears focusing, to look around and see if there was something worse on the horizon. With experience, I realised it was hardly worth a glance.

Only when the intensity, or the density, went up did I take any notice. I might be crouched over a dead seal out on the spring sea ice off the west coast of Signy, carrying out a careful dissection, when its coat would go from spotty black and cream to white due to the fine flying snow particles embedding in the dense fur. If the flurry was a mere six inches above the surface, that's all it did, aside from starting to pile up on the windward side and eddy around the object in its path. A seal was quite a large object on the essentially flat sea ice and the particles drifted over my boots while I concentrated on the job to hand, making sure the black-handled scalpel sliced through the right tissue, or at least didn't slice through mine.

If an eddy whirled up to a height that obscured my view of my cutting hand, I would glance up for an instant at the undulating layer of particles advancing before the prevailing wind, assess the threat, and continue to delve

78

in the plump, steaming interior of *Leptonychotes weddellii* on behalf of science, or so I believed passionately at the time (I still believe it, but with much less passion and a bit more cynicism). Telling stories of heavily embellished incidents came to be my stock-in-trade. At least I could give my mates a laugh and, more importantly, be seen to laugh with them. All part of the bonding process, which was critical in a tiny, enclosed community cut off completely from physical contact with the outside world.

~~~

In the three months that I had been acting as sealing inspector in South Georgia, I had been on virtually every beach on the island that had Elephant seals, which were the quarry of the sealers.

Sitting down firmly on a hump of tussock grass which, with hundreds of Black-Browed Albatrosses, covered the scree-ridden hillside below me, I slumped over to catch my breath after the rushed scramble to achieve maximum height in the shortest time, lest the *Petrel*'s hooter would call me back, pre-empting my effort to reach the glacier's end moraine. The *Petrel* was one of the former whale catchers that were used for sealing that year. The others were the *Phoca* and the *Albatross*.

I had galloped up the slope, fighting my way through the often six-foot-high tussock. As my heaving chest slowed, a sense of relief and achievement came over me. I smiled inwardly, my head came up, and I gazed down to *Petrel*'s diminished outline anchored off Peggotty Bluff. The sealing crew were tiny on the beach, their work punctuated by the crack of the .303 rifle; another Elephant bull bit the dust. Was this the future for this pristine world – the crack of rifle fire, and wildlife, tame to the touch, lying in bloody pools on beaches otherwise untouched by man? But this beach had been touched by a very special man: Ernest Shackleton, the leader of a very special group of men. And during my last days on South Georgia, I was to come close to touching the fame of my hero.

I gazed eastwards and down the fjord. The rifle fire faded into the background. The sun was in the northwest. We were in the southern hemisphere, yet I found it hard to accept, having spent all my life expecting to see its blazing bowl in the southwest at this time of the day. The fjord was virtually mirror calm, or what passed for mirror calm in South Georgia. There were just a few 'willy waws' (mini-cyclones) rising up and sweeping down the fjord to dissipate a couple of hundred yards further on, leaving the sea's surface ruffled but soon to be restored to its shiny self. While I watched, it sparkled with the pulse of solar fire, reflecting off the snow and ice-covered cliffs and hanging glaciers down this most magnificent seascape which stretched to the horizon.

When I lifted my left hand, it was as if I could touch the snow-capped peaks at the entrance, at least a mile away. I was in a fairyland of sun, sea and ice. Then my scientific instincts came to the fore and I lifted my binoculars, always around my neck, right-handedly twiddling the central focus, and the distant horizon jumped out at me. The elements making up the landscape zoomed into view – the Southern Ocean pounding against the cliffs at the entrance, the cruising growlers bobbing beneath the glacier fronts, the swirling, long-winged, pencil-thin silhouettes of Petrels and Albatrosses, lifting and gliding on the air currents, all picked out by the glinting rays of the sun.

I put down the binoculars and took in the view. For the first time in my life, I became aware that beauty existed beyond the hills and hollows of the female figure. That landscape, as such, could be a thing of beauty. King Haakon Bay glowed with its intrinsic splendour, despite, or perhaps because of, its icy demeanour. It was a moment of maturity; the flash of synapses that signalled an inner revelation – beauty is all around if only one can see it. The world is beautiful, not just its constituent parts: its waterfalls, glaciers, mountains, forests, beaches, seas and skies.

I took a deep breath, inhaling the purity of the scene. It was beautiful in its own right, as were the elements that made it up. That synaptic flash may have been the moment of conception of my lifelong interest in the conservation of the natural world. Or, at least, it turned my eyes away, if only momentarily, from the introverted view of a callow youth to a vision that something existed beyond my immediate self-interest.

I stood up, refreshed, and turned and faced the other way, up and across the glacier that led to what is now called the Shackleton Gap. In his time, only a rough draft of the map of South Georgia's interior existed. Duncan Carse, the BBC radio actor of *Dick Barton* fame, had with his team in the 1950s completed the very first survey, and I had met him on the Grytviken whaling plan only a few days before. All I had was a dyeline print (the precursor of the photocopy) of that preliminary map, with only a few detailed names.

I walked on up to the glacier edge, which was packed with spring snow and looking towards the peaks from where it originated. The last Irishmen to stand on this spot were from Kildare and Kerry, Ernest Shackleton and Tom Crean. They, with Frank Worsley, had sailed in a jury-rigged lifeboat called the *James Caird*, with three companions from Elephant Island. The others were Tim McCarthy, a Corkman; Henry McNish, the bosun from Scotland; and able seaman Jack Vincent.

They had sailed 800 miles across the most turbulent seas in the world, arriving safe, if not sound, in King Haakon Bay on 8 May 1916 after their ship, *Endurance*, was crushed in the Weddell Sea's ice on 21 November 1915. Their journey was beyond endurance, yet they survived and crossed the spine of South Georgia, the first ever to do so, to get help for the remaining twenty-two men left stranded on Elephant Island under the command of Frank Wild.

As is well chronicled, Ernest Shackleton, Tom Crean and Frank Worsley succeeded not only in crossing the island but, months later, they penetrated the pack ice at the entrance to the Weddell Sea to rescue all their companions from Elephant Island. The twenty-two had survived an Antarctic winter with only the upturned lifeboats for shelter: a truly amazing achievement.

A lump formed in my throat. I swallowed it hurriedly. In the mist I could see the backs of three men trudging up the snow slope in front of me, hunched over against the wind, now a gentle zephyr, then a very stiff breeze, dressed in a collection of worn-out raggedy clothes with boots and feet that had survived five months on the pack ice before landing on Elephant Island. They were attempting the first crossing of the island with the most rudimentary of maps and footwear. Thanks to the bosun, McNish, their boots had the screws that had held the decking on the *James Caird*, protruding through the soles, giving them minimal grip on the glacier.

When they landed, they camped at the head of King Haakon Bay, at what is now Peggotty Bluff. From there, they had probably passed the very spot I was standing on. I could practically feel the glow of their passing. I took another deep breath, as if I could inhale the very air they had used. All this reflected glory went to my head. The adrenaline kicked in and the buzz felt great. I had been walking in the footsteps of Shackleton!

It was immediately deflated by two urgent hoots from *Petrel*'s hooter calling me back. I looked down onto the beach. The pile of once-steaming, lumbering, Elephant seals was reduced to a pile of skins and a scattering of naked bloody carcasses, surrounded by a mass of squabbling Giant Petrels. The sea was stained red for hundreds of yards. I took one last glance up the glacier at the receding ghostly figures of the Boss, Tom Crean and Frank Worsley fading into the shimmering light, before hurrying down, battling my way through the tussock grass to jump onto the pram as it pulled away from the beach. My fifteen minutes of contact with the famous may have been over, but the memory still remains, bright and clear.

~~~

Having survived South Georgia and the sealers, I was headed for Livingston Island to lead the Fur Seal Summer Survey along with two companions, Alan Sharman, the met assistant and bird enthusiast, and Pete Hodkinson, the base commander at Deception Island.

Livingston Island is a long, thin island, twenty miles by two, lying NE–SW at 61° south in the South Shetland Islands chain, the continuation of the Scotia Arc, which are the tops of the drowned Andes chain stretching down through South America, and finally forming the Antarctic Peninsula, easily visible across the Bransfield Strait. Livingston Island was discovered by William Smith, captain of the brig *Williams* out of Blyth in England. In 1819 he inadvertently penetrated further south than anyone before him, into the terra incognita that was the Southern Ocean south of Cape Horn.

The island was to play an important part in the saga of the Fur sealers and their Klondike-like rush to grab the furry gold, which at that time covered many of the shores during the brief summer months. The Fur seals were there in their millions. In the 1820–21 season they took 60,000 Fur seals from these western beaches. They killed all the adults, male and female, and left the pups, which hadn't moulted into their first fur coats, to die. By 1825 they had wiped out the entire population of more than a million.

Despite that mayhem, the seals recovered, so much so that there was another onslaught in the 1870s, which finally did the job. Livingston lay still and unnoticed except for the occasional reconnaissance. There had been two in the first fifty years of the century, in 1907 and 1927, by the ever-hopeful Norwegian sealers. No doubt they may have been passing whale catchers this far south from their base of South Georgia.

When the Livingston Island summer party of January 1959 was being planned, I asked for Alan Sharman to be included. We had already spent time together, on the way south from Southampton on the *Shack*, nearly three months in all. I liked Alan and our mutual interest in birds, whether watching or catching and ringing, and the science behind the various ongoing long-term projects – on penguins (for Bill Sladen, an ex-Fid, in the US), on Stinkers, and on Dove Prions (for Lance Tickell in the UK) – meant that we shared a great deal.

We had done so all the way south from Southampton when, on the second morning at sea, we both appeared with binoculars on the bow. Most of us were not up to much that first morning; that was a day of abstinence, as the *Shack* headed out to cross the Bay of Biscay with its usual equinoctial weather.

Pete Hodkinson, the third member of the party, was base leader at nearby Deception Island. Pete had come down on the *Biscoe*, so I didn't know him at all, but he came across as a nice guy. Being public school and having a father a brigadier set him somewhat apart socially from the likes of us middle-class nerds.

Both my companions had Antarctic winters under their belts, Alan at Signy and Pete at Deception, whereas I, much to everyone's disgust, had 'wintered' in Monte – the only Fid in the history of the survey to have done so at HMG's expense! Despite my aborted summer on Powell Island and my spring months in South Georgia, I was very much the inexperienced member of the trio. And while I had been super fit from playing rugby in Monte, my couple of months with a wired-up jaw, coupled with being ship-bound on the South Georgia sealers for weeks, meant my fitness (and experience) on and off skis was at its lowest ebb. To top it off, I had been appointed leader of this summer party, which had not gone down well in certain more experienced quarters.

~~~

The *John Biscoe* landed us at the western end of the island, at Byers Peninsula in January 1959. The three months' supply of food and sleeping and camping equipment had been organised by Pete at Deception, and we had picked him and it up from that dormant (or so we thought at the time) volcanic crater of an island where I had spent a splendid few weeks after the sudden cancellation of the Powell Island trip. Only a few years later, in 1964, and again in 1968, the island disintegrated in a massive series of eruptions, which caused the Argentine, British and Chilean bases to be hurriedly evacuated. Now it is a smoking shell-rim of an island, cooled inside and out by the icy waters of Antarctica.

I looked at the confused heaps of stoves, tents, sledges, skis, and scientific gear. 'Right,' I said, 'let's get the tents up.' We quickly hefted the three eight-and-a-half-foot tent rolls up to a slight knoll some ten feet above the beach. Here the spring snow had melted, leaving a slightly sloping patch of mossy green turf, just enough to erect the three pyramid tents in a neat triangle, their mouths pointing northeast away from the prevailing wind.

With only the slightest zephyr of a breeze blowing, the spreading of the four aluminium legs of the pyramid took a mere few minutes. Piling ration boxes and large stones from the beach on the eighteen-inch flap that ran around the foot of the tent took longer. While that was in train, one of us went inside through the tunnel of the sleeve entrance in the outer tent into the inner, which hung from the pyramid's apex and from the supporting poles, and stretched out the groundsheet. The seven-by-seven-foot groundsheet covered the floor, with a small turn-up flap around the walls. With the constant condensation and freezing, the ground sheet and flap would make an airtight seal with the ice beneath and the inner tent, and would become totally draught-proof.

Once the sleeve was tied on the inside, the tent would also become completely air-proof except for the one-inch-diameter rubber tube that penetrated through the two tent covers near the apex and protruded into the outside, allowing some exchange of air under nearly every possible weather condition. Once the snow accumulated around the base of the tent and filled whatever holes it could find, this three-inch tube became our lifeline. Keeping that air-line clear from being clogged with drifting snow was a vital task if one was not to suffocate quietly during the night. Facing the tent away from the wind ensured that the tube, which was on that side, would not become continually packed with snow. When that happened it guaranteed a wakeful night for all.

I had learnt my lesson on my first solo camping trip on Signy Island when I had pitched the tent facing the best view, and coincidentally into that evening's blizzard. The trickle of snowflakes into the tent from the air-tube had turned into a flood, and meant a sleepless night. So I was particularly conscious of the need for careful consideration of when and how to pitch a tent.

Happily, this time, on Livingston Island, my experience paid off. During ten days of continuous blizzard, I only had to uncork the tube in my tent once, and the build-up of snow within it was so slow that an occasional inspection was all that was needed. Having set up the tents and moved all the fragile gear into the store tent, we chose which tents we would sleep in. Alan and I would spend the first period together in one tent and Pete would live in solitary splendour in the other.

When the camp was set up and everything that needed to be pegged down sorted, we whipped up our first meal of 'new' meat bar and baked beans. The bar was a dehydrated compressed chunk of what one hoped was mincemeat. With a small snow bank a few yards away, it was merely a matter of scraping off the outside two to three inches of snow, which had various bits of moss and dust deposited by the regular high winds, and the pot was piled with pristine snow which, when melted, provided a gut-warming cup of thick chocolate … or was that just wishful thinking?

Sitting outside the tent on the moss bank, damp with spring, watching the small bergs cruising past on the current and feeling totally relaxed after the effort and excitement of setting up camp, provided us all with a deep sense of contentment. A rush of well-being, of gratitude to Him who (with the FIDS) organised it all, as well as a great feeling of companionship, overtook me.

~~~

Alan and I got on remarkably well, despite the fact that he regarded me as a total novice with only a few days' Antarctic camping experience fifteen months previously on Powell Island. He was a veteran, having survived more than a whole year of Antarctic deprivations. But I put up with his derision at my inability to deal with the everyday snow-and ice-survival techniques:

skiing, man-hauling the sledge, fishing in the ice holes, cooking in the tent (this was particularly hazardous since I had never done it before).

In the third week, I decided that leaving Pete alone was not good for his mental health so I dumped Alan out of the leader's tent, and took in Pete. I wasn't looking forward to spending seven days and nights cooped up with him, but much to my surprise we got on well. He accepted that, as a leader, my opinion was worth more than his – an attitude no doubt drummed into him by his domineering army father. I remember him telling me that he applied to be an Antarctic explorer because his father said that it would make a man out of him.

Pete was the kind who believed in the system. He had been to a minor public school for military families, and was all about 'King and country and all that crap', as one of our Lancastrian companions cynically put it. He preferred to be called Peter, but nobody would comply, just to annoy him. This was standard practice; if you showed a preference (or a weakness) for this or that, everyone would go out of their way to see you didn't get it.

Of course this was mostly done with humour and the desire to get a rise out of you, but sometimes if someone was having a bad hair day, the boot might be put in that bit further. You soon got used to it and learnt to ignore any sort of taunts or cracks, knowing that if you reacted, the group could home in on you like vultures, hovering just out of arm's reach, to watch the fun.

~~~

Having set up camp and organised the food and gear, we started looking for the elusive Fur seals. We spent the first two weeks walking the coastline of the peninsula and found nothing, though we did penetrate Cutler's Cave, discovered by the FIDS survey party the previous year.

The island had hardly been visited and not even accurately surveyed until Dr Hugh Simpson and his FIDS party from the Hope Bay base at the tip of the Peninsula landed there the season before us. In fact, it was Hugh's pressure in London that got our trip off the ground and into the field. He had discovered not merely a few Fur seals scattered along the coast, the first seen in the Shetlands since the nineteenth-century sealers, but cooking pots for boiling up blubber and skinning implements.

Most importantly, he had discovered a cave across which a small wall had been built with rocks and whose cracks had been filled and were stuffed with seal skin and fur. It had been roofed with whalebone ribs, which probably had been covered by seal skins. Careful digging out of the snow-covered floor revealed a cooking ring of stones and seats of giant whale vertebrae, one of which was carved with *B. Cutler Sch*. Back in Britain, Hugh's research revealed that Benjamin Cutler had been the first mate of the brig *Williams* out of Blyth in England, captained by William Smith, in 1822.

Could this have been an overwintering campsite? Were these the first people ever to winter (and survive) in Antarctica, more than seventy-five years before Otto Nordenskjold? His expedition in 1899 is officially recognised as the first party ever to have wintered there. All these questions remain unanswered. What was badly needed was another excavation with more time and a whole summer to chip away at the permafrost that maintained everything – the soil and the sealers' remnants – frozen solid year-round in its icy grip.

Now all we had to do was find some living, breathing – to say nothing of breeding – Fur seals. We hoped that when we got to Cape Shirreff on the north coast and to the east end of the ice cap, some twenty miles away, we might find some of the adults that Hugh and his party had seen the previous year. But first we had to check out Cape Shirreff. To get there we would have to man-haul all our gear: tents, food and equipment. Hugh had said this was easy going and we didn't need to take a Husky team, which they had done.

I looked over at Alan. He was struggling with his boots, welded as they were to his barge-sized feet. At these high latitudes, the low temperatures, even in summer, would probably have meant instant frozen feet, as insulation in these boots was pitiful. For climbing purposes – and we spent a vast amount of our time scrambling around on slopes of rock-strewn scree – they were virtually useless, having practically no depth of grip on their rubber-ridged soles.

Fortunately, some of us recognised their true value early on and either found or scrounged some other, often old, footwear from departing Fids. But more often than not this was not before minor frostbite to toes or heels had provided sufficient pain and irritation to paint the air blue with comments regarding FIDS, or boot a nearby Elephant seal. That always worked. Of course, booting Elephant seals didn't happen often – there weren't all that many of them around close to the hut.

Nor was it as dreadful as one might think. It was really like kicking a partly inflated rubber tyre, and could be harder on the toes than the tyre. The sight of them dropping off six-foot cliffs onto sharp boulders below without stopping to think about it made one realise how well their thick blubber layer preserved them from more than the cold and how impervious to pain they seemed.

~~~

I wasn't looking forward to several days on the ice cap. I was totally unfit, having spent the last few months sitting around on sealers' boats in Grytviken, inspecting their bloody trade of killing Elephant seals. I had struggled to keep up with Alan and Pete as we covered the Byers Peninsula during the previous weeks.

I had never man-hauled anything anywhere, and now we three would be pulling a 500lb-sledge, up the icy slope of the ice cap to its crest. The two lads thought it would only take two or three hours in the morning. Although they were fit, having spent their last year in the Antarctic, they had no experience pulling a fully loaded sledge. Though we spent the afternoon deciding what gear to take and how much food, it still took half of the next morning to transport everything to the foot of the ice cap, load the sledge and secure everything on it.

We got into our lamp-wick harnesses at 11 am and started the pull up the slope. After thirty minutes of huge effort, we had gained about 200 feet. I decided we should do what was then blindingly obvious and portage the gear in much smaller loads up the slope. This meant unloading three-quarters of the load and dividing it into four parts. The system worked but it took the rest of the day. We were fortunate with the weather and, for once, we had a fine day with little wind or snow. We camped on the crest: not ideal but we were all knackered, me especially. After the hot meat-bar meal, I fell into my sleeping bag and was asleep in an instant.

The next two days were a repeat: packing, pulling with skis slipping continually across the hard-packed ice of the ice cap; camping, but erecting only one tent, crowding in all three bodies; making and eating a hot meal, and falling asleep. By midday on the third day, we were at the point where the downward slope peeled off towards Cape Shirreff. As the slope increased, we were able to climb or cling on the sledge. We thundered down the last half mile and, luckily, ended up embedded in a snow bank without breaking ourselves or anything else.

Once we had dug out the sledge, we hauled it onto the volcanic gravel slope, running towards the sea, and stopped at the first possible camp site. First, we put up the three tents. Next, we melted the snow for a cuppa. Then I proposed we spend an hour or two inspecting the rocky terrain for seals. I was told in no uncertain terms where I could go; tomorrow they might consider it.

I was so euphoric because we had gotten there and I had not fallen on my face too many times that I headed down the slope for the nearest rocky beach. Sweeping the shore with my binoculars in the hope of seeing a crowd of Fur seals, or even one, I wasn't watching where I was putting my feet. Suddenly I stumbled over what I thought was a rock. As I picked myself up, the 'rock' gave a snarl. When I looked down, there was a twelve-inch Fur seal pup in front of me! He was trying to make sense of what had kicked him.

This was the first Fur seal pup recorded south of 60° – the official start of the Antarctic – since the Fur seals had become officially extinct in the previous century. I shouted for joy: fame at last! Now I was going to make it into the history books, if only those relating to Antarctica. And I did. *Nature*, the august science journal, published my first ever science paper, 'Return of the Fur Seal', as did *New Scientist* magazine.

~~~

I had always been interested in birds. At home in Clontarf we lived close to the North Bull Island, a sand bank that had developed as a consequence of the survey of Dublin Bay by the infamous Captain Bligh of Mutiny on the Bounty fame, in 1800. On the 'Bull' and in the estuary of the River Liffey, Dublin's main river, every migrant bird collected at some time or other, often staying for the winter or the summer as the case might be. But birds, in general, were wary. None were friendly, having been trapped, shot and eaten for millennia. So it was a pleasant surprise to arrive in Patagonia, the Falkland Islands and South Georgia at the edge of the Antarctic and find that you could approach within touching distance of most species. And if you sat still, they would come to you, the smaller ones to sit on your boot or hop onto your knee in the hope of finding a morsel to eat on this new arrival into their habitat.

Virtually all the species were completely new to me, aside from the ubiquitous sparrows, and the penguins, which were mind-blowing. There were Cape Pigeons, a sea-going species having no relation to the pigeon family, and Sheathbills. Later, I was to have an intimate relationship with the Giant Petrels, or Stinkers.

There were Prions and Blue-eyed Shags, but I was surprised that Arctic Terns were not on the list. While Antarctic terns were regular, if not commonplace, visitors in the islands of the Scotia Arc, Arctic Terns were, as one might expect, not. Arctic Terns breed in the Arctic, no surprise there, but also in much of coastal northern Europe, dispersing around the Southern Ocean during winter.

Therefore they should be thin on the ground in the Antarctic. So seeing one's first was a pleasant surprise: a shock, even, but a lovely one.

I was on Livingston Island when a bird, flitting amongst the brash ice on the shoreline, caught my attention. I struggled to pull my binoculars from the warmth of my anorak and hastily focused before the ever-persistent lubricant on the joint went stiff and unyielding in the breeze. It was an Arctic Tern, in winter plumage; no black cap, just a dot of black behind the eye and a bright red tip to the bill. It had to be a bloody Arctic Tern, last seen by me flitting along Bull Island beach in Dublin Bay. Flying with jerky wing beats, head cocked and eyes focused on the waves below; ready to fold its wings and crash dive onto the surface for a planktonic morsel exposed by the turbulent toss of the waves.

Here, nearly 9,000 miles south, its attitude was the same, as were its requirements. I watched it travel along the shoreline to be finally lost in the spray thrown up on the next rocky pinnacle jutting out into the sea. I took a deep breath to calm down; my chest heaved, my pulse raced, my breath caught in my throat with the sudden realisation of this vision from my backyard at home. I sat down carefully on an icy boulder and pulled out my field notebook and wrote *Arctic Tern!* along with a brief description, time, date, and place: *10.40, 24.2.' 59, north coast near Cutler's Cave, Liv. 1s., St. Shets.*

A warm feeling spread through my chest. Had they not been reported by Hugh Simpson, the leader of the summer survey party last season? I should ask Pete. But that day, sitting on that rock, gazing at the line of terns on the near horizon, flying beyond the limits of binocular surety, I was content. I could feel the rush of adrenaline at making such a discovery. It provided justification for all the mind-numbing work and endless plodding of this landscape of deadly inhospitality and hazard. For a few moments, the failure to find Fur seals receded and was replaced by the glow of a first for me, and hopefully for Livingston. Just as well I had read Robert Cushman Murphy's two tomes, *Oceanic Birds of South America*, or I would never have heard of Arctic Terns in the Antarctic.

Surplus to Requirements

At the end of our nearly three-month stay on Livingston, HMS *Protector*'s helicopter picked us up and deposited Pete and me on Deception, while Alan was dropped back to the Admiralty Bay base on King George Island. I was to stay on Deception until the *John Biscoe* did her final run around the southern Antarctic Peninsula bases, dropping off expeditionary members to winter and picking up those destined to go to a different base, or head home having completed their two winters and three summers.

Deception Island lies thirty miles from the much larger Livingston Island, in the South Shetland Islands. It is the remains of a volcano, the rim of which is all that can be seen above the sea. It was a major centre of the Fur seal industry in the early nineteenth century, when millions were killed for their skins. When the industry collapsed with the extinction of the Fur seal population throughout the Scotia Arc, the whales were next in the firing line. In 1924 a whaling station was built inside the caldera – it was operated by Salvesen's of Sandefjord until the eruption of Deception's volcano in 1936.

The UK began Operation Tabarin in 1944. It was designed to stop the Nazis from sinking Allied ships rounding Cape Horn at the southern tip of Patagonia. Deception Island became strategically important to the Allies. Warships stationed here could block the southern part of the Drake Passage, the 600-mile constriction of the Southern Ocean between Cape Horn and the Antarctic Peninsula, while the Falkland Islands protected the northern approaches.

Refurbishment of the whaling station manager's house, which was the only building in reasonable repair, provided a ready-made base for the first overwintering party in 1945. The base hut, by Signy standards, was palatial, if a little Victorian. There was wood throughout, with polished floors, now pockmarked from years of booted men tramping through. In the days of whaling none of that would have been allowed; in those days you took your boots off on entering the manager's house.

Spacious sitting rooms led to a series of bedrooms, which had two to four bunks when we arrived. Though this was private territory for the long-stay Fids, the short-term visitors just bunked down wherever they pleased.

Once I settled in, my first urge was to travel to the Argentine and Chilean bases much further in the caldera. This could be done by a small boat called a 'pram', and an outboard in good weather, but the weather was set to stay windy and the choppy sea in the caldera would end up in one's lap. A cold, wet trip was not recommended, even in an Antarctic summer. So my friend Alan, the assistant meteorologist and a birdwatcher, and I geared up for the walk along the shore where permafrost lay side by side with warm springs and fumaroles.

The base had built a small loo-sized hut over one of these springs. We went and had a look. The bubbling hot pool give a cosy feel to the interior. I dipped a finger in, and yelled. The bloody temperature must have been close to boiling point. My finger ached like hell and I felt just as stupid. Alan grinned – he had been to Deception before. I blew on my finger to cool it off. Alan suggested I stick it in the snow outside. Plunging my red-hot finger into cold white snow might provide immediate relief, but the damage to the scalded tissues could not be good and extended the pain for a much longer period.

If they wanted a bath, the intrepid new boys were expected to run naked from the hut to the boathouse, fill up the bath with the near-boiling water, cool it down with snow, then plunge or leap in, luxuriate, and finally sprint back over the volcanic gravel to the hut. I don't know how many of the uninitiated fell for this, but I wasn't one of them. After all, this was my second year and I was no longer wet behind the ears. I took off my boots and socks and, luxuriating in the feel of the warm gravel, I, without thinking, stripped naked, took two strides and plunged into the freezing sea.

As you can imagine, it was a totally new experience. However, one plunge was enough; within twenty seconds I was out again, standing on the warm gravel trying to reduce the shivering and get dressed in my full Antarctic gear. I was urged to do it again by the onlookers. Not bloody likely. I might be an Irish git, but there were limits. That evening, I was the talk of the ship. People were shaking their heads in disbelief, and muttering that only the Irish could be so stupid, but many of the Fids were wishing they'd had the courage to do the same thing.

We left Deception the following day. It was a worthwhile trip, if only to give the new boys a touch of the extraordinary range of land and seascapes that Antarctica had to offer.

In Forster's Bay, the flooded interior of the not-so-extinct volcano was to blow up again in 1969. The deep blue of the ocean reflected the sheer sun and ice-clad cliffs that surrounded one on every side. These Antarctic vistas were jaw-dropping but the *Biscoe* didn't linger long; the following morning before breakfast she was out through the Bellows two-six, as they say in the Royal Navy, down the Bransfield Strait, and onto Base B at Rothera Point, via the Gerlacke Strait, which lies between the sheer cliffs of Anvers Island and those of the Antarctic continent.

~~~

My second time in Deception I arrived at Whalers' Bay in the austral autumn, in March, at the same time as a team of huskies. They were to be lodged here temporarily until it was decided where they should winter. They couldn't stay at Deception as the fractured crater rim of an island was no place for dogs. Base D, as it was called, was not a survey base and had no food stores for feeding ravenous huskies all winter long. Also, there was no colony of seals lying out on the autumn beaches or winter sea ice that could provide five pounds of meat a day, every day, for seven hungry huskies.

As a visitor, I had no official function at the base, and being a biologist, I was asked to look after the dogs. I fed them their meat bars every evening, their only meal, and soon became their best friend. They would bark, jumping to their feet and wagging their tails every time I came near the wire span they were tethered to. In those weeks of waiting to move on, I grew very fond of each and every one. It was, after all, the only form of overt affection available, and having just spent nearly three months in a tent with one or other of my two companions, any object that could be petted and would wag its tail back at you brought an important psychological boost.

That changed one day in March, when a signal arrived from head office in Port Stanley in the Falklands: the team of huskies was surplus to requirements. Nobody wanted them. We should arrange for their demise. Everyone on the base was up in arms. Appeals bounced back and forth between the office in Port Stanley and the base. All sorts of proposals were mooted. I suggested giving them to the nearby Argentinian or Chilean bases, which were only up the coast from us. That was not geopolitically possible; the Argies would take them and publicly exploit the cruelty of the perfidious Brits. I even proposed letting them 'escape' to find their own salvation. But the base commander disagreed. He would be blamed and they'd only hang around our base or maybe turn up at one of the other bases and be returned, much to HMG's embarrassment. No, they would have to be killed. The decision hung over all of us like a very dark cloud.

98

After about ten days of our refusal to carry out the order, I was called into the base commander's office and shown a signal instructing him to instruct me to carry out the deed. I would not be on base during the coming long winter nights and months of isolation, when the blame game could boil over and provide a flashpoint for violence. Anyway, I was a bloody biologist, wasn't I, used to killing animals and collecting their bits. Hadn't I shot a couple of Leopard seals down on the beach a few days before and spent my days grubbing around in their insides? I protested loudly, to no avail.

The base commander said I could take it up directly with Johnny Green, the operations officer, but I should remember he might consider the refusal of a direct order as insubordination and send me home. The *Biscoe* was due. It was supposed to deposit me at Signy, in the South Orkneys, en route to the UK, but could be ordered to take me home. I was appalled at the prospect.

I hurriedly left the base, forgetting my gloves, and rushed along the beach to try to find some calm. I ended up at the derelict whalers' graveyard. I sat on the gravel beach, plunging my bare hands below the windswept surface, to feel the volcanic warmth less than six inches down. After a few moments, my hands started to warm up and the constriction in my chest began to ease. My instinct was to tell Johnny Green to get stuffed, but the previous year I had caused him a lot of trouble, complaining about the lack of planning for my studies of the Fur seal. I was given to understand that he was a cantankerous little git, huffing and puffing self-importantly. I'd better cool it. Go for a long walk and think it through. I went back to the base, grabbed my anorak, woolly hat and gloves, and headed out for the Bellows, the entrance to the volcano's caldera from the South Atlantic.

An hour later, I was sitting on the crater's rim, looking northeast towards Livingston, the island that I had recently left, and southeast across the

Bransfield Strait towards the mountains of the Peninsula. Edward Bransfield was Irish and they had named the strait after him. I felt totally alone, isolated from my companions, not just physically but ethnically, culturally, religiously and emotionally. I was a practising Catholic and, despite the abuse I had taken at every turn about being 'a bog-trotting Paddy', I had never had my religion thrown in my face. Of course, religion was not something young men in their twenties think or talk about much. This was the first and only time when isolation, that insidious and dangerous feeling of being utterly alone, raised its ugly head. I felt crushed.

The breathtaking vision from the crater's rim of the Bransfield Strait, with its multitude of icebergs, large and small, and the towering mountains on the mainland of the Antarctic continent, made no impression. I stared down the cliff at the waves pounding the base and contemplated my dilemma. All I could see was smiling whiskered faces and wagging tails.

Eventually I got up, my rear end heading towards frostbite, and made my way back to the base hut in time for lunch. I got lots of inquiring looks but no one was so crass as to mention the subject. Everyone knew what I was being asked to do, and I knew that if I did it they would feel not only relief, but also sympathy.

After lunch, I went to the base commander's office and asked for the rifle. Silently, I was handed a .303 and seven bullets. I left, not having exchanged another word. It was a blistering cold but sunny day. I grabbed the short length of rope that was used as a lead by anyone taking a dog for a walk. We couldn't let them run wild, as they would pursue, catch and eat anything that came across their path. Deception had a large breeding population of penguins, mostly Chinstraps with a few Gentoo, so there were always disjointed streams of penguins heading across the beach into the sea, or to the rookeries, high on the slopes of the mountainous rim of the caldera.

I walked down to the span. As I approached, all the huskies leapt to their feet, looking hopeful. No, it wasn't feeding time but I did have the lead; it was walkie-walkie time. I stopped and surveyed them. They were mangy looking, moulting, their coats old and bedraggled, but all in good form, hoping they would be the one. Where would I start? Should the leader be first or last? I walked to the end of the span. The last one was the smallest. Poor Sam. I clipped the lead to his collar and released him from the trace that bound him to the heavy wire span. He leapt with joy, pulling me along the beach, trying to get me to run in the loose, volcanic gravel. I was in no mood for any sort of running. The strap of the Lee Enfield was across my chest, the gun banging me on the back every step of the way, reminding me of the reason for walking the dog. To add to my distress, the bullets bounced around in my pocket, never letting me forget what I'd been commanded to do. I walked mournfully around the curve of the beach. Sam, having failed to get me to raise my pace, had given up pulling, and was strolling along, investigating any scrap that might turn out to be edible. Normally this would not be tolerated. But today was special. I was not likely to deny him the chance to sniff at every bit of debris washed up on the deserted beach in the South Atlantic.

My pace slackened. Slowly we approached the cliffs near the Bellows. Here the piles of volcanic gravel, which covered everything, even the glaciers, since the last eruption of the volcano in the 1870s, gave way to large boulders that were eroded from the rim. We reached the rim and arrived at the cliff edge. Sam squatted down, laying his head and paws across my feet. I carefully tied the lead around a large chunk of pumice, less than a yard from the edge. I slipped the.303 off my back, moved back a yard or two, and started loading. I pulled back the bolt, allowing the first bullet to spring into the breech. I drove the bullet forward and clicked the protruding knob of the bolt down. Now all I had to do was pull the trigger. I looked at Sam and stopped. He was straining on the lead, trying to come closer, to take part in this new game. Was I going to throw this long stick for him to chase? He gazed up at me, his head to one side.

I peered down the barrel aligning the gun sights, my heart in my throat, pounding. Sam wagged his tail, his head cocked, a grin of anticipation on his lips. My hands trembled. I couldn't do it; I couldn't guarantee even at three feet that the first bullet would do the job properly. Anyhow, I was shaking too much. No, Sam deserved better than that. I had to be sure that the inch-long bullet, travelling at 4,000 feet per second when it left the muzzle, would, in that instant, do the deed. Having served loyally all his life, Sam would die instantly, no longer a logistic liability.

I gritted my teeth, lifted the gun, moved closer, swung around and fired. My last glimpse of Sam alive, head cocked, looking hopeful, was one that I can still see clearly today. He slumped to the ground. The echo of the shot reverberated around the cliffs. I was stunned, unable to hear anything except the blast of sound that heralded the death of Sam.

I dropped the rifle and knelt down beside him. I had shot a lot of seals, for research and for feeding man and beast, and knew what a heavy-duty bullet like a .303 could do. Sam had a surprisingly small entry wound below his left eye, and only a thimbleful of blood on his cheek. But when I lifted his head and saw how little was left of it, my stomach erupted and my undigested lunch mingled with the blood-soaked rocks. I wept.

Later, I wiped my eyes and with a quick heave sent Sam into the depths. When I had the nerve, I looked over the cliff, hoping against hope that he was not lying on the rocks below, but had found a watery grave. I sighed with relief. One down, six to go. A long and painful day lay ahead. By the time it was all over, I had missed dinner – not that I could have eaten – and I didn't appear around the base but took to my pit.

The following day, I kept out of the way of all the base members, deciding instead to travel to the Argentine base, less than three miles away, scrambling across the heavily crevassed intervening glacier en route, not caring about the outcome. I returned to base late that day. No one, to this day, has ever mentioned the missing huskies.

~~~

With all the to-ing and fro-ing to Signy, Powell, Port Stanley, Montevideo, Buenos Aires, South Georgia, Deception, Livingston and Hope Bay, it was eighteen months after heading south that I finally got to settle into a base – on Signy. Arriving there in April 1959, after a hectic austral summer on the last autumnal call of the RRS *John Biscoe*, was a bit strange. I was the only one disembarking; all the others who would winter on Signy had arrived in the spring. Even though I had travelled down with some of them, it had been over a year since we last met. They had not seen a ship or a new face for nearly eight months, and for some this was their second winter at Signy.

Isolation in a small group forces bonding, and any new arrival inevitably has to cope with being considered a blow-in, disrupting the group's set routine, however legitimate their purpose. Also, it was vital to know everyone and their roles, both official and non-official, their likes and dislikes, their strengths and weaknesses. Should I just barge in, elbowing my way into the group, or tiptoe around the periphery, seeking a gap in the group's cohesion to slip silently in, taking a back seat? I thought about this for all of five minutes on my way in on the *Biscoe*'s lifeboat.

Pete, the base leader, met me on the jetty amid all the hurly-burly: I was surrounded by my personal gear – suitcase and a rucksack – which had followed me around and looked a bit like its owner, bruised and somewhat battered. Bernard, one of our assistant meteorologists, was a small Bedfordshire man with twinkling eyes above burnt and chapped cheeks, all framed by a bushy beard and a wild mop of hair, which for the occasion of the ship's visit had been slicked down with a generous dollop of water. He wore a freshly washed khaki sweater sprinkled with a series of neatly mended holes over a khaki ex-army shirt that had seen better days.

His khaki trousers, likewise, showed the effects of a summer spent chopping up seals, hauling boats, cooking, gashing and all the other chores that everyone took turns to do. Walking and scrambling over the crags and moss banks around the island was for him, like most of us, the way to find relief from the cramped, in-your-face existence for nine young and very different men living within the four walls of a wooden hut measuring a mere seventy by twenty feet.

'I'll show you your pit,' Bernard offered, after his silent handshake. 'Thanks, it's great to be finally here,' I grinned in reply. 'I see it's still there,' I added, smiling at the sign over the door. Bernard, glancing up, looked somewhat surprised. He had forgotten its existence but for the new boy, it was a welcome sign of anti-authoritarianism. The carving depicted two rampant bull Elephant seals facing each other, their noses fully inflated; a scroll underneath had a neatly carved motto: *Semper in Excreta*, it proclaimed appropriately. Subsequently, during a visit by the governor, who was having 'a jolly' before heading back for the UK and retirement, someone foolishly pointed out – with pride – the motto over the front door. Astonishment, then barely suppressed rage was the response. Through gritted teeth it was ordered down. This wasn't the sort of place that he presided over; it was an insult to the FIDS, the FCO and, by implication, the Queen herself. It was removed, but of course went up again directly after he left. But it was taken down for any ship's visit until some wimp of a base leader concerned for his future career got rid of it. The history of that sign would be interesting. I'd love to put it over my front door!

~~~

The first day after the departure of the *Biscoe*, and my second day on base, I climbed the hill past the met screen and the radio tower to Berntsen Point, and sat down on what became my favourite rock. The scene before me was breathtaking. Looking north across Borge Bay, I identified the headlands and islets that would become familiar landmarks in the months ahead: the Mirounga Flats and the outer islets all the way to North Point, an imposing hill with a sheer cliff guarding the southern side of Normanna Strait.

Across the strait, the glistening white mass of Coronation Island filled the horizon west to east. It had two massive glaciers, the Laws and Sunshine glaciers, which were more or less directly opposite Signy. They shone with reflected light like two megastars, their tumultuous, mile-wide fronts dissected into massive ice stacks riven with blue-green clefts that set off their brilliantly white faces.

I put up the binoculars and they seemed to fill the screen, even though they were at least ten miles distant. The perspective in Antarctica was amazing. The air was so crystal clear that, on good days, it seemed you could touch the horizon of mountains even if they were thirty miles away, as was the east end of Coronation. A mere five to ten miles was nothing. It made travelling both a joy and a hazard. The spectacle of land, snow-covered from its peaks down to the sea, never failed to impress me. Nowhere else in the world, aside from Greenland and the other high Arctic islands, could you see this. It was as if you had cut the top 10,000 feet off the Himalayas and dropped them into the sea.

Everywhere south of the polar front at the 60th parallel in the west Antarctic, this was the scene: the archipelago of the South Orkneys at 61°, the South Shetlands at 63°, and the continental Antarctic Peninsula from 64° to Alexandra land beyond the Antarctic Circle, all gleaming white (in those days) and mighty. Mount Barnes in the Orkneys was the highest peak at 5,600 feet; in the Shetlands it was Livingston Island's Mount Bernard, also just under 6,000 feet (or so I thought at the time). On the Peninsula, the backbone of the Andes reappeared, with peaks of over 7,000 feet. Mount Vinson in latitude 78° is the highest, at over 16,000 feet.

Since those first days, all this area has been, for me, Himalayan in character. The vision of Coronation glistening white, from head to toe, has never left me, never diminished. This pristine land was barely touched, and still effectively unpolluted by man's effluent. But for how long?

These days, the tourist ships have arrived. What next? Hotels? They're on King George Island in the South Shetlands. Still, the continent itself, aside from the scientific bases, is pristine. What about a road to the South Pole? One is being built by the US, connecting its base in McMurdo Sound in east Antarctica with its base at the South Pole. And then what? Bus concessions and Big Macs?

During those first days on Signy, we were more than fifty years away from those possibilities. The future was peace. The Antarctic Treaty had just been negotiated; 'Antarctica for Science and Peace' was the hope. In Antarctica, even at the height of the Cold War, the Russians cooperated with the US and everyone else. That first blissful day, I thought I was in heaven.

106

The silence was breathtaking, catatonic. Only occasionally did a bird call from Factory Bluffs behind the base. Soon they would be gone and the silence would be complete. Except, of course, for the calving glaciers off the Sunshine opposite, which I imagined I heard, or the infrequent gentle boom coming from the face of our own glacier at the back of Borge Bay, which seemed to calve very infrequently, or else had decided to do it quietly so as not to disturb our tranquillity.

Gradually, day by day, I absorbed more of the landscape, more of the sound of silence, as the moods changed, the wind wound up and calmed down, the snow fell and the temperature fluctuated up and down the scale. All these interdigitating variables provided a kaleidoscope of environmental tones which wafted over me, silent and content on my ice-cold rock. It became my place for reflection, for thinking through problems, for coping with the ways of the rest of the great unwashed below in the hut, quite literally in most cases. I should have photographed that rock, and should have it up on my study wall to provide, in more turbulent times, memories of coping, of tranquillity, of peace.

Once settled in, there was time to explore. The sites with concentrations of wildlife were an immediate draw for most of us, especially me. Right behind the hut was Factory Bluffs, so called because of the remains of the Norwegian whale factory that existed between 1912 and 1926 and whose site we occupied. When the base on Signy was first opened in 1946, the remains of the dilapidated factory building with the plan, onto which the whales were hauled up and butchered, still existed. In our day, only the remnants of the wooden plan survived, as well as a wooden storage shed which we demolished so we could use the material to build a hut for the biologist on the west coast. However, despite the demolition, the material never made it to the west coast, at least in my time.

At the highest point, 630 feet, I could see the whole island – to the east the mountains at the end of Coronation and the Michael's Pinnacles guarding Lewthwaite Strait and Powell Island where I had spent my first full day in the Antarctic more than eighteen months previously. Sitting there surrounded by ice and icy landscapes, the sun in the middle distance, the intimations of loneliness and of solitude grew on me. If I looked due west, the next landfall would be Heard Island, south of Australia, up to 10,000 miles away. Looking east, there was Marion Island, which was nearly 7,000 miles distant. Cape Horn and desolate Tierra del Fuego were 1,000 miles to the northwest, and to the south it was a further 1,900 miles to the edge of the continent and the British base at Halley Bay in the Weddell Sea.

It was a similar distance again to the US South Pole base. Could I, in winter, walk to the Pole from here? I had always believed I could. Recently satellite imagery has confirmed that, in the Antarctic winter, the Weddell Sea's solid pack ice reached up to enclose the South Orkneys in bad (or good depending of your view) ice years. So I was right all those years ago, sitting on an ice cap on Signy Island. I could have done a Shackleton and walked to the Pole, at least in my youthful imagination.

There was no doubt we were isolated. Once the last ship, the *Biscoe*, left in April there would be no visits from anyone until the spring; in fact, that year it was December before we saw the *Biscoe* return due to the winter ice, which was one of the worst on record. Gazing at the immensity of the surrounding space, which if you looked up included the whole of the cosmos to infinity, I found that my stature, which at five foot eight and a half I thought of as adequate, diminished rapidly: first to the size of an ant, but it soon shrunk even further to the size of a pinhead. I couldn't think of any

Fergus record high jump 1952

Port Stanley Cathedral,
Falklands, November 1957

Approaching South Georgia
Island 1957

RRS Shackleton alongside
Southampton dock 1957

*Elephant seal skins, South
Georgia, September 1958*

*Flensing an Elephant seal bull,
South Georgia*

111

Whaling, a bloody business on Grytviken,
South Georgia, September 1958

Sea ice on approaching Signy Island

*Semper In Excreta - Motto for
Signy Island base 1957-60*

Signy base camp, Summer 1959

*Fergus and Bernard hard at
work - coal supplies, Signy 1959*

*Pete (Tink) Mander knackered after
unloading coal sacks, Signy Island,
November 1957*

114

Grand National on Weddell pup
at Signy

First day of Winter Jolly approaching
Coronation Island, dog sledging

115

*Alan Sherman, Signy 1958,
ringing Giant Petrel chick*

*Charlie le Feuvre and friendly
Weddell pup, Signy 1959*

Fergus on last day in field ringing Giant Petrel chicks, west coast of Signy, April 1960

Source of drinking water, Signy Island, Winter 1959

*Charlie and fresh rolls for breakfast,
Signy Island, Winter 1959*

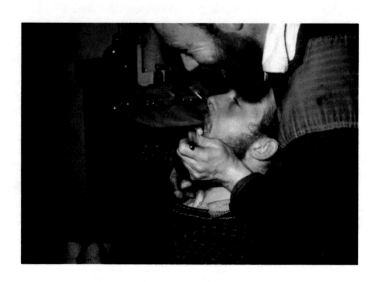

*Fergus performing dentistry on the base
leader Jim, Signy Island, Winter 1959*

George doing his annual wash,
Signy Island, Winter 1959

Wintering Group mid-Winter June 1959
Back row left to right – Bill Mitchell (DEM), Ron Pinder (Radio Op),
Jim Young (Met), George White (DEM), Charlie le Feuvre (Radio Op)
Front row left to right – Bernard Harrison (Met), Jim Stammers (BL,
Met), Karl Kenyon (Gash Hand), Fergus O'Gorman (Zoologist)

Mid-Winter dinner and dance
at Signy

Christmas dinner Base H 1959
Left to right – Roger Filer (Met), Bernard Harrison (BL, Met), Fergus
O'Gorman (Zoologist), Ron Pinder (Radio Op), Pete (Wink) Mander (Met)

Fergus painting a bull Elephant seal, Signy Island 1959

Macaroni male, Signy Island

121

Adélie and chick

Chinstraps

*Alan and Tinks' graves on
Admiralty Bay*

Shackleton's grave, South Georgia

123

Ceremony of Commitment on ice at 68 degrees South of
Denise Comerford and Fergus, 2015, below Antarctic Circle

visible object smaller than that. But in the context of the size of the earth, even the head of a pin was inadequate to represent our diminished stature.

I sat there, seeing the millions and millions of human ants scurrying to and fro around the distant world of which I was not a part. And to what purpose? We nine were totally isolated from that frenetic activity, in body and spirit. The Earth we all inhabited was less than a pinhead in our galaxy, which was only one of many in the infinity of space. That day, more than at any time before or after, I felt a powerful sense of the Lilliputian nature of the world we live in, and of our frantic and largely futile efforts to conquer our earthly environment. I felt for the first time, but not the last, the extent of the arrogance of mankind, top dog on this earthly heap, or so we believe, but nowhere in control of our destiny, being hurtled into outer space in an expanding universe to an uncertain future with climate change and other environmental disasters already upon us.

My cold rear end reminded me that I had done enough navel-gazing for one day. I got up and retraced my steps through the soft snow back to base, and Charlie's hot rolls.

~~~

We young males, none that long away from our mothers' administration, tended not to care very much about our appearance. Pong was the defining criticism. No one ever commented on one's attire. Your hair could be untamed, rarely if ever seeing a comb. Burnt or cracked lips, cuts or bruises never even got a sympathetic glance. I can remember only one occasion when my visage was commented on. It was my gash (housekeeping) day, and I had been out on the plan. As I was about to sit down for lunch in the kitchen, Jim looked up from slurping his soup and said, 'I see you've had a bloody good time.' This brought a hoot of laughter from the rest of the team.

I went next door to the dorm, the only place with a mirror. Peering at me from that cracked and peeling square was a wild, dirty, red-bearded face flecked with a network of spots of dried blood, making me look like I had some hideous rash. Dried blood is not all that easy to remove, especially when you have no hot water. Some judicious use of a pumice stone was required. I returned to comments such as 'Who's the new lad, then?'

We were filthy most of the time. Some people washed their hands and face for Sunday lunch. Some even boiled up a kettle on the Aga and trimmed their moustaches and beards when a particular party was being held. The Queen's birthday was one such occasion. Of course, in true British fashion, this wasn't her real birthday, which was 21 April. No doubt the thinking was that if she dropped off the tree, the powers-that-be wouldn't have to remember a new one; they'd just cross out Queen and insert King.

For this occasion, some people – those with middle-class upbringings – dressed up. Some even put on ties and what passed for a suit. The rest, including myself, came as they were. This was a political statement of sorts, though few of us had strongly held political views. Politics was off the agenda for discussion, as was religion. Of course, that didn't prevent religious or political slurs from being slung around, but that wasn't a discussion, merely a statement. Only one really heavy political discussion took place, which I remember as George 'having a black'. He ended up in his jenny shed and didn't come out for three days except for meals.

During the summer when there was running water, at least during the day, washing, and even having a bath, was not a problem. The coal-fired Aga ran twenty-four hours a day, 365 days a year. Next to it was a forty-gallon tank full of hot to boiling water, which was piped in from the reservoir up the hill.

So you could, if you wished, have a bath once or even twice a week. But nobody did.

George and I seemed to be the ones who were picked on most. Me because, being a biologist, I spent most of my time in the *merde* anyway. If I wasn't sitting among the foul-mouthed, farting Elephant seal pods and wading through their liquid green or red poo, I was up to my armpits grabbing Cape Pigeons on their nests on the cliff face, or turning over stones hunting for Wilson's or, God willing, the much rarer Black-bellied Storm Petrels, or late at night swooping on Dove Prions, active in their burrows.

All these Petrels – even the tiny Storm Petrels – have a common defence mechanism. When alarmed or attacked, they regurgitate an oily fluid from their crop. That is bad enough, as it smells of partly digested fish or squid. But most of the time they add to that by bringing up their last meal, spewing the lot over your hand and arm if it's in a burrow, or over your face and hair as your head comes over the edge of the ledge on the cliff face. If you combine that with the fresh, and not so fresh, poo splashed everywhere, you can imagine the Van Gogh look I might have at any particular time. And that was before I started dissecting whatever I found to dissect – birds or seals or whatever was the flavour of the day.

One might think that this would require at least a daily scrub. But not me; I merely hung my heavily impregnated anorak in the lab – most of the time it stood up by itself – and just went and washed my hands. As there was no mirror in the bathroom, there was no need to inspect the facial damage. On demand, I would change my jumpers around, leave the bad one to ripen in the bath and then switch it with the only other one I had when it became too much that even I smelt it.

The latrine consisted of empty food cans that had to be carried to the shit heap daily in summer, or taken by boat into the bay, topped up with stones and sunk. Aside from those couple of months of less than freezing temperatures, the now solidly frozen tins were removed more or less weekly and sledged out onto the sea ice. They were left to pile up and wait for the spring break-up to end their life, floating north, east or west into the Scotia Sea or south into the Weddell, to provide nourishment for the abundant marine life. When I first thought about this and visualised the mounds of human excrement pile up in Borge Bay, it nearly put me off eating Charlie's freshly caught and deliciously cooked local fish: some sort of a cod. Its official name was *Notothenia*. If it had an English name, we never knew it.

On only one occasion that I can recall was I prevented from entering the hut due to the odiferous nature of my being. That was when I returned from my very last field trip, having spent a couple of weeks on the west coast of Signy ringing young Stinkers: enough said! The fact I was the biologist allowed me a lot of latitude. 'He's been fucking around inside female seals again,' or some even more ribald comment would always produce a series of smirks or guffaws. The fact that I almost always took it with a grin allowed me to carry on doing it. My attitude became part of my survival stock-in-trade and was much needed on occasion.

George claimed that absorbing diesel oil through his pores was his reason for the aura that surrounded him. How could he tinker day and night with a jenny and not be covered from head to toe with a thin mist of diesel, which over the year hardened into a permanent crust on every surface of his being?

He had sallow skin, black beard and hair, heavy black eyebrows, and a thick black, drooping moustache whose ends dipped regularly into his soup. 'Aaghrr,' he would exclaim in his thick West Country accent, 'that be good' as he stuck his moustache ends into his mouth and, with exaggerated sucking noises, transferred the soup clinging to the greasy ends into his maw.

He would look around grinning, hoping that some disgusted conservative middle-class git would rise to the bait. Nobody reacted; they'd seen it all before, many times. 'Jesus, George!' I rejoined the first time I saw this performance. 'You'll have no need for a packed lunch tomorrow; sure you'll have eating and drinking in that beard, to say nothing of the hatching *hemiptera* larvae.'

~~~

With the exception of George, whose official duties were indoors, and Ron, the radio operator, we all had outdoor work, and everyone had to operate as a gash hand by rotation, which meant doing or helping with any job that needed doing. This included feeding the dogs, acquiring their food by shooting seals around the coast, and transporting carcasses; counting nesting birds, ringing every bird you could catch, banding penguins, tagging seals.

Darning of socks, jumpers, shirts and even trousers was a constant sight on base. It was mostly an evening activity when everyone collected in either the sitting room or the kitchen, depending on the outside and the inside temperature. On really cold days, with strong winds, the kitchen was the place to be. The Aga provided 70°F of heat except in the early morning, as it was let run down during the night. These were the only two rooms that were heated in the base hut.

There was no heating in the dorm, except during exceptionally cold weather. The outside temperature had to be -10°F or lower (42°F of frost) before it was even contemplated. The temperature in the dorm had to drop to 0°F (32° of frost) before a fire was permitted. A small open fire made little or no impression on the ambient temperature, especially at the end of the room where my pit lay beneath the window. It was all about conserving coal, in case we had to spend another year in isolation, with no relief ship able to get in.

For those who had done national service, darning was not a new event in their lives. That didn't mean that they could do it properly: some never learnt, and few darns were commonplace except on socks. Everyone recognised that keeping one's feet intact was essential, and valiant and repeated efforts were made to cope with the wear and tear of continually walking over rough ground in the summer, or ploughing through snow and ice for the other nine months.

I had never done anything akin to national service; in fact, I had hardly ever been away from home on my own except for the first European Catholic School Olympics in Manchester, in my last year of secondary school. I'd extended this into a walking holiday in the Lake District, the scene of so many of my favourite outdoor stories, including Arthur Ransome's *Swallows and Amazons*. How simple life was in those days. For that trip, my mother had laden me down with piles of socks so that my rucksack bulged with extra everything, most of which came home unused.

At home, I saw my mother darning socks; my sister Joan had to learn how to darn, but not us boys. That was women's work, as was washing-up, cleaning the house and ironing everything, to say nothing of cooking three meals a day. The only time I saw my father in the kitchen doing anything other than eating was on Sunday mornings when he fried the breakfast and brought it up to my mother in bed.

So the mystery of darning for me was just that. I had to learn from scratch and never could get a nice neat web over the expanding hole. George was no better. 'This is women's work,' he would fume. On one occasion, he struggled ineffectively with a particularly large hole in the heel of one of his few socks. He glared, muttered and howled when he stuck the needle in his thumb, finally throwing the sock on the floor and departing in a foul humour for his den in the jenny shed.

We subsequently heard him thumping around in the attic. Finally, he reappeared with a satisfied look on his face. He was carrying the leg of a long-john. Sitting down, he proceeded to cut out the knee which, through use, had a slightly rounded appearance. He then sewed it over the recalcitrant heel hole as we watched, fascinated. Once finished, he held it up triumphantly. George had done something that all those middle-class mammy's boys, stuck in the traditionalist groove, couldn't do. By thinking outside the box, he had come up with a technical breakthrough of profound proportions. Pulling on the sock, he proceeded to walk around shoeless for the rest of the evening, casting admiring glances at his left foot. Several people tried to follow suit, but few persisted.

~~~

By the time I arrived on base in Signy, George had one winter under his belt – which he let us know several times – and was 'an old hand', dispensing opinions to the new boys, usually at variance with the other Fids on base. His anti-establishment attitudes appealed to me and we got on well, despite our very different cultural backgrounds. 'What's that?' he asked one day, as he peered at the semi-translucent object floating around in the fish tank in my lab. 'It's a ctenophore,' I replied, as I tried to concentrate on catching the multitude of tiny shrimp-like creatures sculling around near the surface with a small hand net.

''Ere, what did you call it?' he said, his thick accent coming to the fore. 'Ten-oh-four,' I repeated. 'Sounds like one of them cops and robbers movies,' George remarked. 'No, it's spelt C-T-E-N-O-P-H-O-R-E,' I said, treating him like the country yokel that he wasn't. 'Oh, it's a fucking jellyfish. Why didn't you say so?' I looked up, my amazement showing. 'You're not as thick as you look,' I responded, with a smile. 'Not going to the university doesn't mean you're thick,' he muttered.

George had left school early and ended up as an aeronautical technician working for British Aerospace in Bristol, just down the road from his home in Wotton-under-Edge. When the punch-ups between the workers and management became too much, he left, deciding life in the Antarctic would be a bit less stressful. But it was not to be. His rural background combined with his trenchant workers' rights views guaranteed that the rest of us explorers – middle-class urbanites – would use him as the essential bringer of mirth, so important to our closed community of nine souls isolated for more than a year in the Antarctic. He became the butt of every joke and the focus for many mealtime rants about the state of British life.

He had a passing interest in biology and used to drop into the lab regularly. 'What are you wasting your time and the British taxpayers' money on today?' was often his opening gambit. The ten-o-four was a gelatinous mass about the size of a cocktail sausage with line upon line of tiny arms beating a rhythm along its body, repeatedly flashing a rainbow of colours as they propelled it through the water, this way and that, looking for what it might engulf.

'Can I have a closer look?' George asked. I gave him a magnifying glass and he peered in, nose pressed to the tank. 'It has bloody millions of them,' he exclaimed. 'Do you mean its pseudopods?' I said with a supercilious sneer. George glared. 'They're called cilia, you silly bugger.' 'Well done, George – full marks, I'll make a biologist of you yet.' 'Not bloody likely. I banth be fiddling with no gonads and tings like you be doin' all day – it's not

132

Christian,' he declared, stalking out without a backward glance.

~~~

Once autumn had arrived and the temperatures took a dive, the outdoor loo, just a bucket in the store shed, fifty yards from the back door, was abandoned for the indoor loos, both of which were only used when pooing was essential in the vicinity of the hut. This was to reduce the odour to manageable proportions, and was an unstated, and unconscious, early form of recycling before organic recycling was ever heard of.

Of course to pee or not to pee was never the question, once we were outside, and one of the oldest living organisms on the planet – the moss banks – were the recipient of our excess mineral and liquid waste. I often wondered if this was one of the reasons for their luxurious growth, in this particular place. In summer we spent as much time out of doors as possible, so there was not much accumulation in the indoor loo. This loo was inside the back door but outside the heated area, which was closed off by another door. As a consequence, even in summer the loo area was fresh to bloody freezing, so much so that only the dedicated stayed any length of time; it was mostly in, a fast down of the trousers, down with the long-johns and underwear, a quick sit on the cold wooden seat, a quick wipe, up anchors and away.

One bitterly cold winter's evening, with the temperature below zero degrees and a wind that would freeze any exposed digits, most were enjoying the warmth of the coal fire in the sitting room and the blast of Ella Fitzgerald from the gramophone. As usual after one of Charlie's exceptional meals, replete with spotted dick and every crevice filled with tea, the needy one in our group 'Ben', departed in due course to the loo, in what was effectively the porch. This was part of his daily cycle, his biological clock pinged and he went with whatever paperback novel he was reading at the time. Some considerable time later, I heard a scream.

Being nearer the kitchen door I was out first. In half a dozen strides, I jerked open the door to the porch and beheld Ben hopping from one foot to the other, his pants around his ankles, holding his willy, which was dripping blood. Horrified, I asked if I could help hold it for him while he pulled up his pants. 'No, you fucking well can't,' he muttered through his clenched teeth. 'What happened?' I asked. 'Oh, fuck you,' came the reply. Ben did another shuffle trying to pull up his underwear, long-johns and trousers all in one go with one hand. The loo seat was exposed and there, on the lip, was a blood-smeared icicle.

I knew instantly what happened. Ben had left half his willy stuck to the seat. 'Don't bother looking, you can hardly see it. It's minuscule. He'll be joining the castrates in St John's choir, when he gets home.' Guffaws, peals of laughter came from Charlie.

I ran down the hall to the bathroom, grabbed what looked like the cleanest towel, rushed back and gave it to him. 'Wrap it up in that,' I said, grabbing his shirt and pulling him to the office where I took the first aid kit. Pulling it open I extracted the smallest bandage I could find. 'Now wrap it up in that.' I handed him a couple of plasters and left him to it. What had happened was that Ben, sitting in the loo having a quiet read, had dribbled urine which in those temperatures, probably twenty degrees of frost, froze solid – attaching the end of his willy to the aluminium rim of the can beneath. When he eventually stood up, the foreskin, stuck to the rim, had ripped.

There was one last thing to do. I rushed into the kitchen, grabbed the kettle simmering on the Aga and dashed to the loo, lifting up the seat. There it was, the bloodied icicle protruding from the rim of the tin can. I poured hot water over it and it slid into the depths.

134

Claustrophobia and Peace

On that white continent I developed a sense of isolation I'd never before felt. We men were thrown together, not chosen for our compatibility, and living very closely in the harshest environment on Earth with no hope of rescue should anything, mental or physical, go wrong.

Claustrophobia also became an issue. Almost everyone had base-bound jobs: Jim was the base camp commander; Ron and Charlie were the radio operators; George was the jenny man, Bernard and Bill were the met men. It was really only Jim and Ken (the general assistants) and dog-team drivers and myself who had official reasons to be away from base, though dog driving was a bit of a flimsy excuse seeing as all the survey work on Signy and on the large island opposite, Coronation, had been completed.

But I had no trouble finding an excuse to leave base. Birdwatching, even in the depths of winter, when there was not a sign of a bird, was the common euphemism used. 'Ah! If it isn't the early bird! If you catch one, bring it back for tea.' These, and more ribald comments, were made as I headed out, binoculars prominent, into the winter's gloom. I always hoped I would see something – a seal, a long-lost penguin, anything – but mostly I went, as did the others, to get some personal space. To get away from the interminable sameness of the conversations, the chewing over and over of the same old arguments, the jokes repeated ad nauseam. A new twist on an old story, a new event, especially some new cock-up, or even a rehashing of an old one, would become the event of the day during the long winter, which extended from late autumn to early spring.

Once outside, we went our separate ways. Each of us had a favourite place for peace, where a familiar scene or objects greeted you, silently. In time, these places seemed to develop a glow or, more miraculously in such an environment, a warm embrace. My favourite spots were scattered. The closest was on Berntsen Point, the southern point of Borge Bay, and only a couple of hundred yards up the hill east of the base. If I felt like making more of an effort, or needed to expel accumulated angst, I would climb Observation Bluff, 364 feet high, and directly behind the base.

If I was really in need of a long period of peace and freedom from human contact I would, from spring to early autumn, head for Gourlay Peninsula, the most southerly point on Signy on the east coast. That required a couple of hours' hiking but was worth it. It was the site of the biggest Adélie penguin rookery and it was a delight. My spirits lifted as I approached. Just the sight of the miniature black and white figures trudging up the slope from the sea was enough to put a smile on my face. We all reacted similarly. They were comic, and often hilarious, like waddling nuns in black habits and starched white fronts. Being allowed to laugh at holy nuns was a new and delightful experience. 'He's been to Gourlay,' was the cry I'd get as I arrived in for tea, still smiling broadly from the experience. Several times I suspect my sanity was saved by the Sisters of the Order of the Adélies at their retreat on Gourlay.

Once the ship left in April, taking the summer visitors or last year's over-winterers home, the sense of isolation grew. At first, it was a relief; now there were only eight others. What bliss: more room in the hut, a new choice of bunks, freedom from all the panic of the past few weeks, writing up and typing the summer and annual reports with two fingers. And we'd had to cope with the frisson of excitement that ran through those departing. The anticipation of being homeward bound after two years and eight months of isolation from family and friends.

Everyone sighed with relief the day after the *Biscoe* left, though the previous evening the final farewells had brought a few lumps to a few throats. Not surprisingly, George was the one who articulated the relief. 'Good riddance,' he growled, glad to see the back of all the bustle of loading and unloading, and all the curious who came ashore and poked around into every nook and cranny, some staring at the over-winterers as if they were in a zoo. George made sure everyone knew that his jenny shed was off limits to any 'tourists'. This was, of course, long before the first tourist ship hove-to in Borge Bay ten years later, in January 1969.

In those first few weeks, the sense of being alone with nature and a few companions grew, and was welcomed. Everyone settled down, pottering around, each preparing in his own way for winter.

There were no squabbles, no bickering and there was even little ribaldry. We were all on our best behaviour, tolerant and helpful. That status quo would gradually deteriorate as winter loomed over the western horizon.

~~~

I woke up one morning at 8 am and my eyes felt as if they were glued shut. I didn't try to open them; I just lay there on my back, listening. Not a sound. The dormitory was as quiet as the grave. No heavy breathing, grunting, coughing, or rustling of bed clothes, sleeping bags or whatever. That was unusual. What day was it, I wondered. Days were merging into one another. Then I remembered it must be Sunday, as last night there had been a booze-up. By agreement, booze-ups only happened on Saturday, unless there was a special reason: a birthday, or a Charlie cook-up special. He delighted in cooking and we enjoyed the fruits of his labour. Being the only teetotaller, I tended to wake up earlier than the rest on Sundays as I'd probably gone to bed earlier than most.

There were no sounds outside either. A lull in the regular winter gales was always welcome and I lay there, luxuriating inside the ancient sleeping bag I'd found stuffed under a loose floorboard in the attic. It smelt like it had been there since the hut was rebuilt in 1953, but then again, everything smelt, as we did ourselves. If it wasn't musty, it was the smell of stale sweat, or seal blubber mixed with blood, or husky body fluids, that added to the melange of odours of varying stages of fading putrefaction.

Outside my sleeping bag were the three or four used blankets purloined from the regular store, as well as a piece of quilt that had been used to wrap up some of my scientific equipment that had been repacked in South Georgia for onward transporting to Signy. Inside the sleeping bag was another matter. Having removed my trousers and shirt, I would have rapidly donned pyjamas over my long-johns and string vest. They would be tucked into another pair of socks and track suit bottoms, but not the top. That had been lost in one of the many ship transfers. Instead, I had a left-behind Shetland sweater, which resembled the string vest because of the many holes in it. This completed my night-time ensemble.

Though no one had yet enunciated the principle of three or four layers being the most efficient form of insulation, we had worked it out, more or less, as a result of trial and error. It meant, of course, that I took off clothes when I got up in the morning rather than the other way around. For much of the winter, I wore gloves in bed: the silk ones I had for handling scalpels and suchlike in the freezing lab or outside dealing with the huskies, or otherwise dossing around during the winter months.

On this particular morning, things seemed to be different. It wasn't only the sound of silence; my eyelids were refusing to function. My lips, nose and eyes were outside the insulating effect of the sleeping bag and were stiff with cold. No elasticity. I grimaced as I tried to move them. Sneaking a few fingers out through the gap left in the mouth of the laced-up bag, I tried to rub my eyes. I encountered a rim of ice crystals and realised that my lashes were frozen together. My whole face – at least the parts exposed to the ambient air – was covered in hoar frost. The beard surrounding my mouth had turned into a forest of icicles, where my breath had condensed and frozen. My nose felt like a larger icicle – rigid, unyielding and cold as the asshole of hell. And if that wasn't enough, my chest appeared to be constricted, or at least weighed down.

I squeezed my eyelids, breaking the connection. A bit of vigorous rubbing and one opened, then the other. I squeezed my nose after peeling off my glove with my teeth; I couldn't get my other fingers out through the gap. Anyway, my nose could only accommodate so many fingers. Gradually, it started to warm up and flex. Soon, I was flexing the nose cartilage back and forth. So it wasn't frostbitten and would not come off in my hand; not this time anyway! I pressed my lips together and broke off the icicles, yanking out a few hairs.

With my freed fingers, I worked at the knot on the lacing of the bag. It too was covered in glassy ice, due to my breathing on it all night. In between freezing and melting it had developed into a thumb-sized chunk of ice. Wrapped in my hot palm, it started to melt dribbling ice-cold water onto my neck. Having melted the ice, I then had to prise the knot apart. It finally gave up the ghost and I was able to poke my head out. I glanced down the bed. I couldn't believe what I saw. Beyond the forest of melting ice – which was my beard – was a pyramid of snow, probably six inches high, sitting on my chest.

How in God's name had it got there? My first thought was that my friendly companions had deposited it there. But, no, it was far too fluffy for that. It looked like it had descended from above. But seeing as I had the bottom bunk, and there was an unoccupied bed above, that seemed an unlikely explanation. I brushed most of it onto the floor and struggled out from under the pile of insulation. The dorm felt unusually cold. I looked at the thermometer hanging just inside the door – it was -17°F, which meant there was 49° of frost in the bedroom.

A puff of wind, laden with snow crystals, caressed my cheeks. I peered at the nearby window. Yes, there was a crack running down the inner pane. And as far as I could see there was a hole punctured in the outer pane, with a small piece of ice jammed into it. Well, that explained the pile of snow on my chest, but how had a piece of ice been propelled against the window? I peered up the snow slope that ran down the back wall of the base hut. There, for all to see, was a track of hard-packed snow, a result of some idiot skiing full tilt down the slope, swerving to a stop at the last moment and, in the process, throwing up a pile of snow and ice against the wall of the hut.

I took a deep breath. Of course, that idiot was ME. Never having skied before, I had set out to teach myself. My fellow Fids weren't interested in recreational skiing. I had envisioned myself careering down the Alpine slopes at full speed, and this was the start of it. But here and now, I had a problem. Once it became known that the bloody bog-trotting reckless Paddy had put everyone's life in danger with his antics on skis, I would never live it down. Ever after I would be known as that fellow who nearly wrecked the hut at Signy and endangered his fellow Fids. But what could you expect from the 'effing' Irish? It would follow me around for the rest of my life. Better do something quick about it before everyone was up and about.

I donned my outside gear and rushed, quietly, out of the hut, grabbing the snow shovel that was used every day to clear the four or five foot wall of snow that accumulated overnight. I crept around till I reached the mound of the ski track below the cracked window and hurriedly demolished it. I finished it off by prising out the piece of ice stuck in the pane. Having casually put back the shovel, I sauntered into breakfast and declared, with a straight face, 'I see we have a cracked window in the dorm – I wonder how that happened?'

~~~

A clatter was coming from the kitchen. I stuck my head around the door and saw Charlie engrossed in the production of fresh rolls for breakfast. It was his week on cook, thank God. I remembered now why I wanted to wake up early. It was first come, first served and hot rolls with butter – of which we had an endless supply – and strawberry jam, just now starting to be rationed, were not to be missed. In fact, all of Charlie's meals always got a full house. (Our diet was generally high in proteins and fats to keep us warm. I remember putting huge lumps of butter in my tea to raise the fat content!)

Usually George would be sitting there, looking expectant, well before the usual time. Breakfast in winter never started before 8.30 am and could run to 10 am or later, with people arriving in dribs and drabs, but not when Charlie was on cook. I never discovered where he learnt to cook, but he definitely had flair. For a group of virtually insatiable young males, it was a welcome skill, especially as most of us were mediocre or worse.

We had penguin eggs, which not everyone took to. Unlike hens' eggs, the white wasn't white at all but completely transparent and much more viscous than the white of a hen's egg. But the more striking difference was that the yolk was a bright red with a touch of orange. If you broke two eggs into the pan, you had these two yolks staring at you like two large, bloodshot eyes.

The look wasn't the only off-putting thing about penguin eggs; once cooked, the whites were like rubber, your teeth bounced off them and it required considerable chewing and gulping of large drinks to get them down. Eventually, I gave up. While the penguin eggs still lasted – we had collected several hundred – I only ate the yolks, which, like all fresh food in the Antarctic, had a strong and distinctive flavour of their own. A large pot of porridge was a sine qua non for breakfast, with lashings of sugar and large chunks of butter added. Powdered milk was made up daily to cool it down and change the tea from a mahogany brew to a deep tan colour. Some cooks only turfed out the tea leaves once a day; others were more fastidious and changed them twice daily.

It was a relief after the struggle with the rubbery eggs and the boiled brew to get your teeth into the bread, and Charlie made the outstanding effort in the baking department. He was up at 6 am on his week; heating the yeast and getting it to ferment, mixing it with the flour and butter, waiting for it to rise, bashing it back, cutting it into palm-size pieces which, when rolled into small balls, rose in the cooker end of the Aga into a yeasty layer of enticing rolls.

Once they had risen to the appropriate size, Charlie would transfer them to the main oven, by which time we were all sitting around expectantly eating our porridge course. Charlie would open the oven door, allowing the yeast-filled scent to fill the kitchen. If you hadn't already been salivating, you certainly were then. Most people made a real effort to provide edible bread, though not everyone succeeded. Bernard tried to produce something that wasn't a dense mass of unrisen dough, but despite endless efforts and coaching, he never really succeeded. His bread rolls were either rock hard, whence they became dangerous missiles to be fired around the kitchen, or delightfully crispy on the outside and just glutinous lumps of dough in the middle.

142

Charlie tried to iron out the quirks in Bernard's dough-making technique, as we all did. Even the more challenged cooks, such as myself, tried. After all, bread was a huge part of the diet, in both volume and calories. One deep breath inhaling the delightful aroma of baked flour and yeast and one's chest inflated and a swoon was not far off. With Bernard, the smell was there but after the first few goes, we learnt that the consistency left something to be desired. We also learnt not to bite down in case a cracked tooth was the result – and that would be a disaster as it meant a visit to the biologist, there being no dentist (we had no official cook, or medic, or dentist – we all had to rely on the bloody biologist for that, except me, as nobody could offer to do it for me).

On the days we threw our leftovers out, our resident birds, white Snowy Sheathbills, acquired their daily bread outside our window. I couldn't open the kitchen window so I would have to rush out from the baking temperature of the kitchen (75–85°F) to the comparative warmth of this particular sunny windless day, with the temperature in the shade hovering about zero. Being in an open-necked shirt with rolled-up sleeves to cope with the kitchen heat, and wearing raggedy slippers, the sudden drop in temperature to 43°F took my breath away.

Having deposited Bernard's roll (known as 'BBB', Bernard's burnt bread) on the windowsill, and in so doing flushing the ever-present Paddies, which scampered or flew five or six yards away, I scampered back inside. (The Paddies' official name is the South Atlantic or Snowy Sheathbill, *Chionis albus*. When I asked, one day, why they were called Paddies, I was told that, like the Irish, they are always in the shit!)

The first Paddy returned and cocked its head at the roll. Having eyed it up and down, it gave a tentative peck. Was this brown, round object just an

143

odd-shaped, discoloured penguin egg? It had another go. Two heftier pecks made no impression on Bernard's bread roll. By this time, the cohort of resident Paddies had come close, forming a dispersed semicircle consistent with their place in the pecking order. The second in line stepped onto the windowsill.

Simultaneous pecks and the roll shifted and teetered on the brink. But there was still no sign of an impression. The leader of the pack, determined to demonstrate his place at the head of the queue, aimed a vicious side-swipe. This was enough to propel the BBB off the sill and onto the snow, where it made a small dent. Here it nestled, surrounded by the rest of the lower ranks.

A few quick pecks before the boss and number two arrived. Still intact, but the concerted tap-tapping of bills on the brick-hard carapace set it popping and quivering from the repeatedly frustrated Paddies mutt-mutting to one another as they each tried to make an impression. All of a sudden, the kinetic energy it was accumulating from the repeated pecks propelled it up and out of its resting place on top of the snow slope, which ran towards the hut's gable end and the back door.

It was chased by the Paddies, who, every time it slid to a stop, pecked it further down the slippery slope. Within a few seconds it was moving apace, followed on three sides by a muttering of Paddies. Finally it stopped, where it was mobbed. Everyone pushed and shouldered their way in to tackle the recalcitrant object of their desires. Still the BBR refused to give up. Finally, numero uno jumped on top of it, both feet driving downwards, claws extended. Surely this would be the coup de grace?

I strained to see out of the window for the result. After several hefty pecks between his legs, the boss stepped off, causing a retreat among the lesser fry. He stood front-facing, chest puffed up with the effort, the adrenaline coursing through his veins. He cocked his head to the right, levelling all the malevolent vision of his left eye at the object, which was now half sunk in the snow, its slightly burnt underbelly open to the next attack.

One more effort – half-hearted – and still no joy. The boss turned away in disgust, lifted his tail of soiled white feathers and squirted a stream of white and pink shit in the direction of the BBB. Enough said! For some time afterwards, I looked at Bernard's rolls with a somewhat jaundiced eye and a slight queasiness, which was soon, however, dispelled by hunger.

As one got used to eating everything that resembled food, especially if it was served up, all prejudices, foibles, dislikes were laid to rest – hunger, after all, is the best sauce. But for me one remained off limits. No matter what, I couldn't stomach rice pudding. One day, we were sitting around the kitchen table waiting to be fed. The conversation was, as was often the case, about food. I was recounting the food served at an upper-crust 'do' in Montevideo, which included large bowls of savoury rice as the staple. I had looked around in horror – where were the potatoes? I put a small spoon of the rice on my plate while all round me were piling into it. The first tentative taste – three grains balanced on my upturned fork – was not unpleasant, a slight greasy olive oil taste. Out here, it came in tins as creamed rice. But no matter how hungry I was and no matter how hard I tried, I couldn't get past the first spoon.

I had visions of my mother standing over me with a large spoonful of hot gooey rice and raspberry jam, stuffing it between my clenched teeth. This used to happen two or three times a week. All I had to do was see a bowl of rice pudding and I could see Mum, her face fixed in a gritty smile, cajoling the heaped spoon into my reluctant mouth. But otherwise I licked my plate, sometimes literally; good manners went out the door the first day we sat down in Tonsberg House on Signy together.

~~~

While meals brought us all together, to exchange experiences, to catch up with the news, to plan a sealing expedition or a bird-ringing foray, we also brought our daily frustrations to the table – the jenny was acting up; a finger had been sliced by a scalpel due to a moment of carelessness; there was a radio blackout due to adverse weather; the bread was like cement bricks; Garth, that effing Husky, had got off the trace again and chewed up the seal skin being cured on a wooden frame; or that bloody Leopard seal off Gourlay had taken one of our oldest ringed Adélies. The list was endless.

It was a challenge to carry out the work programme without incurring serious injury or death; a challenge to cope with the isolation, both mental and physical, along with the hothouse existence in the hut. Bodies were never more than a few paces apart for days or weeks on end; we were locked into a tiny world thousands of miles from what passed for civilisation. The only peace was to be found by taking a walk on the wild side: in summer to Gourlay Peninsula where the Adélies thrived, or to the freshwater lakes to see if the ice had retreated enough for some macroscopic life to appear, or to North Point to sit among the Blue-eyed Shags and watch their entwined necks displaying courtship and new life to come.

For me and most others, Gourlay was the place of recuperation. It allowed for relief from the stress of daily intimacy with companions with whom one had surprisingly little in common, except that we were here to do a job and wanted to survive to tell the tale.

From early spring, when they first appeared, Gourlay was the place for the Adélies: trudging across the sea ice until autumn, when the last young stood around with downy feathery tufts still clinging to them, hoping perhaps

146

for a last free meal from their mothers before plunging into the hazards of the South Atlantic. Fewer than 10 per cent would survive and return to breed.

When really stressed, I would head for Gourlay on the days when I wasn't working there. I would stride into the centre of the colony, avoiding as far as possible the grasping beaks of sitting males and the upright rush of mates with flailing rock-hard flippers, battering me from ankle to knee. With practice, most of the more aggressive birds could be avoided.

Arriving at the centre of the colony, I would sit down – out of reach – and immediately the agitation would decrease to its usual level. The colony was never quiet, but the cacophony of sounds made one feel just like someone watching the milling urban crowds in New York or Hong Kong, where normal communication was (and is) often an impossibility. Within moments the antics of this crowd of scruffy waiters in tails would bring a smile, and soon loud laughs.

An hour of this and the return trip to base was one of remembered giggles that persisted for hours after, and often into the following day. Thank God for Adélies. Surprisingly, the Chinstraps and Gentoos, which were also plentiful, didn't raise the same belly laughs. Nor did Rockhoppers, Macaroni, Jackass, Kings or even Emperors, however interesting they were en masse at their rookeries.

In winter, no such outlet existed. With the declining sunlight and the increased frequency of storms and therefore hut-bound days, people tended to slink into a favourite nook somewhere in the hut with knees drawn up; psychologically in a foetal position. People even volunteered to read the met instruments, which were a hundred metres up the hill from the hut, as this forced you to get out. I regularly went the extra two hundred metres to Hut Point.

147

Even in a stiff breeze with the temperature well below freezing, I would admire the landscape of dense, unmoving pack ice between Signy and Coronation, and the swathe of spectacular ice pinnacles released from the Laws Glacier opposite and trapped in the Sound for the winter. There were icebergs of every size and shape, the most prominent being castle-like turrets.

Here there were no tabular bergs – the flat-topped cubes cut from the Filchner or Ronne Ice Shelves more than 1,000 miles away, which had broken off years ago, maybe even in the time of the crushing of Shackleton's *Endurance*. Ever since then, they had been cruising the Weddell Sea to be finally pushed out by the circulation into the circumpolar currents of the Southern Ocean, and moved north to bounce off or collide with the chain of islands across their path – the South Orkneys or the South Sandwiches. Here, in the sound facing north between Coronation and Signy, they were few and far between. From the south coast or high up on Signy's ice cap and looking south, my binoculars showed their outlines on the horizon.

Aside from the frozen sea embedded with icebergs, the changing light on Coronation provided some of the variety of cloud formations over Mount Nivea, which came right out of the sea, flanked with glaciers and huge cornices, and packed with pristine snow. I could see myself schussing down those steep slopes. I could even hear the hiss of the snow under my skis, even though I wasn't able to ski down the slope behind the hut and arrive in one piece!

Sitting there on the rock-hard frozen snow ridge of sastrugi (a series of low ridges formed on level snow by wind erosion) that sometimes built up at Hut Point allowed one to both admire the majesty of nature and feel one's own insignificance, and that of mankind. How long these thoughts lasted depended on the temperature of the nether regions. Sometimes I would return

148

to the hut and strip to my long johns and string vest and toast my backside against the Aga until it glowed, blissfully.

There was even more bliss when Charlie was in the kitchen, producing fresh hot yeast rolls. I still salivate at that thought.

Tragedy Strikes

I had only just settled in my winter base on Signy Island in the South Orkneys in early April 1959 when the news of the tragic death of my friend Alan Sharman flashed around the Antarctic.

I was devastated. I didn't learn the details of Alan's death during the remainder of my time in Antarctica; I didn't want to go there. It wasn't until the following year, when I was working in FIDS HQ in London and participating in the Royal Geographical Society's fifty-year commemoration of Robert Falcon Scott's death on the way back from the South Pole, that I met Russell Thompson, who had wintered at Admiralty Bay in 1959, when Alan had died. When I asked him what had happened, he hesitated and seemed reluctant to explain. After much pressing on my part, he finally agreed to tell me the story.

Alan was proud of his mountaineering skills, learnt in the RAF, and he regularly took off to explore King George Island beyond the base camp on Admiralty Bay. Most of his colleagues weren't interested or had other jobs to do that kept them close to base, so he mostly did this alone. He would take one of the old huskies that had accumulated there from other bases to live out the remainder of their lives.

This particular day was unusual; it was windless, with a blue sky, totally different from the normal weather, which was windblown and overcast. Alan headed up the icy slope towards Peak Melville, the highest mountain on the island. He hadn't climbed it yet, and this was the day to do it. With him was Russell Thompson and two huskies, Eddie and Nadia.

As Russell described it, the going was tough and icy. Part of the way up the slope, Eddie was trying to gallop ahead when he lost his footing and slid down the slope, possibly knocking both men over. Alan fell head first down the icy slope and Russell went down feet first. Unable to stop, they both went over a thirty-foot high snow cliff at the end of the slope and fell onto the rocks below.

Russell was stunned and when he came around he discovered Alan had cracked open his head and was covered in blood. Russell had damaged his back and shoulder and had difficulty walking, but he made it back to the base to get help. They got the Nansen sled (named after the famous Norwegian explorer) and hooked up the dogs to go back to Alan. When they got back to where he lay, they stripped open his anorak to see if there was any sign of life. Despite repeated pounding on his chest, there wasn't a whimper from his lungs and not a whisper of a heartbeat. They levered his body onto the sledge and headed for home.

The base leader, Mike, immediately drafted an urgent message to FIDS HQ in Port Stanley and Dick tapped it out on Morse code. All the other bases heard it too, and the airwaves were full of condolences and questions of how and why. No one knew the answers and Ken determined that he would cover the ground again in the morning to see if he could ascertain any facts for the inevitable enquiry that would be required both by Alan's family and by FIDS HQ.

Though it wasn't the weekend, the base leader broke out the booze that evening to provide some solace for everyone to celebrate Alan's life. That went on late into the night until, by general consent, the booze was locked away and all fell into their bunks to greet the nightmares that crowded in. The following morning Russell headed up the hill with Dennis 'Tink' Bell in tow, to try to get the facts about Alan's demise before the next storm of snow and ice obliterated all traces of his passing. It was as stated: Alan had been killed by a freak accident.

152

The atmosphere at our base was unlike anything I had experienced: no noise, no conversation except in whispers. Mealtimes were a hushed affair until four days later when Ron, the radio operator, announced that Alan had been buried. That seemed to break the logjam; everyone started talking at once, announcing their plans for weeks ahead. We all wanted to put Alan's death behind us.

~~~

The day after the news of his death came through on the evening radio schedule, I went off early and walked towards Gourlay via the ice cap summit. I hadn't climbed to the top before and sitting there, absorbing the sea and landscapes, looking southwest to where, 600 miles away, Alan had died, the unforgiving nature of this environment struck me perhaps for the first time. Someone close had died. He was twenty-four, my age.

Everyone knew Alan and he was the only Fid with whom I had a strong rapport. We had got along on board the *Shack*; his birdwatching enthusiasm and expertise had been a great help on the three-and-a-half-month voyage. His official function was as a met man, having done a six-week course at the Met Office in Tolworth. I had hoped that he would join with me as an assistant on the Powell Island summer mapping survey. Cecil Scotland, the Belfast man, was stuck with me. He had a five-man team, including three mapping surveyors and a geologist, and having two new Fids would increase the hazards tenfold and slow down the proper work on mapping Powell Island for the very first time, he said. He, and they, weren't going to do anything that might lose them their place in the history of Antarctic exploration. So Alan had stayed behind on the Signy base and I had to carry out my scientific programme without any assistance.

He spent his first Antarctic winter on Signy before being transferred to his new base, Admiralty Bay, on King George Island, where he was to spend his second winter. After he had been picked up at Signy, and Cecil and the rest of the Powell Island party had been dropped off to spend the rest of the summer there, we headed to Hope Bay to reach its abandoned base, and put in a new lot of Fids for geopolitical reasons. The Argentines had a year-round base there called Admiralty Brown, named after the founder of the Argentine Navy, who was Irish with family from Mayo. They had recently bolstered their contingent there with several army families, one of whom reputedly had produced a child, which they claimed was a first for Antarctica.

We arrived at Admiralty Bay for a quick visit, to drop Alan and the all-important mailbags for the wintering Fids, the first mail from their families since the previous year. As soon as the stores were dumped on shore, we were off to Deception. Before we left, I caught a glimpse of the two crosses on the hill above the base hut of two Fids who had died there – Eric Platt in November 1948 and Ronald Napier in March 1956. It was then December and we were due to be in Port Stanley for Christmas. Sometime in the New Year 1958, I would sail south again to pick up Alan from Admiralty Bay, and Pete Hodkinson from Deception Island, and head for Livingston Island for a Fur seal survey.

Only when Alan died did I realise how little I really knew about his family background. I found it not only difficult but, in fact, impossible to write a letter of condolence to his family. It wasn't until a year after I returned home and was working up my scientific results in Charing Cross Hospital Medical School that I ventured to connect with Alan's family. I went up to see his parents in Bedfordshire, a very difficult visit for all of us.

~~~

Almost exactly three months after Alan died, there was another tragic death

154

among our group, this time that of Dennis 'Tink' Bell, on 26 July 1959. Again, it happened on the familiar route from the base hut over the ice cap to the other side of King George Island. Tink had traversed the route at least a hundred times. He had two ski poles with him but he wasn't wearing crampons and didn't have a rope. So when the snow bridge on the glacier he was crossing gave way, there was nowhere for him to go except down.

When he didn't show up for lunch an enquiry elicited the response that Tink had been seen crossing the glacier. That provoked as anxious discussion, which ended in an agreement to go look for him. The climbers geared up and headed for the glacier crossing. As soon as they saw that the ancient snow bridge had collapsed, they feared the worst. One of the group, who was roped up, crawled to the edge of the crevasse and peered into the depths. 'I think I can see him, he's down about sixty feet,' he said.

The rest of the rescue party crawled up to the edge. Mike, who appeared to be the leader of the group, looked around and said, 'Who is prepared to go down?' Two or three hands went up, reluctantly. Mike, still peering into the crevasse, saw some movement. 'Tink! Tink! Can you hear me?' he bellowed. Everyone who was staring into the crevasse saw Tink's gloved hand move, and a faint sound issued from the depths. 'Jesus!' exclaimed Mike, 'he's alive.' The hard bit was going to be getting him out. Not one of the party on the glacier, or at base, was an expert climber. Alan had been their only expert. Mike started shouting down the crevasse to Tink, trying to ascertain how injured he was. Any broken bones? Was his back OK? All these factors would affect the rescue, which was going to be very difficult.

Tink was jammed on what appeared to be a wedge of snow, beyond which the crevasse disappeared into the depth for at least another hundred feet. How stable was his position? Could it take another body? The walls of the crevasse were ten feet apart at the surface, and narrowed continually down to where Tink had become jammed. This would mean getting him roped up before the hoist, a difficult if not impossible task. Dealing with an unconscious body in the depths of the glacier would be a mammoth task.

Mike continued to shout down to Tink. As time went by, he seemed to be more conscious. He was muttering and trying to lever himself up into a sitting position, back to one icy wall, struggling to get his knees up into his chest. Once he succeeded in doing this, his mutterings became clearer. 'Throw me down a rope and I may be able to do it myself,' he said.

Mike looked doubtful and turned to the other party members. 'Even if Tink succeeds, how are we going to pull him from the depths?' And then the thought struck him. 'How about getting the dogs?' 'Great idea,' was the response. 'Run back to base and get them to drive up the dogs. Make sure they bring enough rope and sleeping bags for Tink,' Mike said. The early morning calm was changing into an icy gale, which transformed the surface into a kaleidoscope of snow and ice particles that raced across the surface and obscured every undulation, increasing the hazards of travel.

The edge of the crevasse had disappeared, and if it wasn't for Mike lying full length and trying to keep up a shouted conversation with Tink, the rest of the party would have been in danger of joining him in the depths. The messages coming from the injured man seemed to indicate that his upper body was more or less OK but that he had a lot of pain in his pelvic area. He was fortunate that he had slipped feet first into the crevasse, thus saving him from the fatal consequences of hitting his head off the ice-hard walls as he descended.

He had been at least two hours in the crevasse, and the temperature down there was well below freezing. Tink was losing body heat by the minute. Just as Mike looked around in desperation, the Husky team could be heard forcing its way up the glacier. As soon as they arrived and were disentangled from one another and pegged out for the downward return trip, Mike took the two climbing ropes, each about thirty feet long, and tied them together and onto the back of the sledge. 'God, I hope they reach him,' he said.

Mike looked worried. 'Here,' said the base commander who had come up with the Husky team, unwinding another, shorter, rope from around his waist. Once that was fixed, Mike started carefully dropping the end of the rope into the crevasse. It didn't get far, as it seemed to get stuck in every protuberance on the wall of the crevasse. When it had failed several times to go down even twenty feet, somebody suggested that it needed to be weighed down. A hurried conflab failed to suggest anything that might work until Jim proposed that they use his skis. These were lashed onto the rope and let down, descending with a rush until Mike started dropping the rope hand over hand.

When it finally arrived in Tink's vicinity, he struggled to untie the knots holding the skis, but finally succeeded. The skis clattered into the depths. Now Tink had to tie himself to the rope. After an inordinate delay, the group on the surface all shivering violently, word came back from below; 'OK!' The slack was taken up on the rope and with everyone pulling, Tink was gently lifted off the wedge of snow, which had looked like it was going to be his final resting place. Painful shouts came from the depths; Tink's pelvis and lower body was now hanging free. He was in agony. The base commander unpegged the huskies and sledge and started down the slope of the glacier, very slowly.

Several of the base members grabbed onto the nearest Husky's harness to control its pace and, inch by inch, foot by foot, Tink came up out of the crevasse. Ten, twenty, thirty, forty, fifty feet; nearly an hour of hauling and pausing. Now they were coming to the trickiest bit, the lip of the crevasse. The huskies, under the base commander's expert guidance, were straining to pull the sledge with the heavy body attached down the glacier. Inch by inch the rope was emerging over the icy lip of the crevasse, which it cut into, creating a deep groove.

As Tink's head and shoulders appeared out of the depths, it was obvious he was in great pain; muted groans and cries issuing from his blood-stained lips. His life was hanging by a thread; actually a taut ten-millimetre climbing rope, which appeared to be coming from his waist up to his chest and past his face to the groove. It had gouged into the icy lip and onward to the sledge. It was obvious that Tink was barely hanging in there; the excruciating pain of his nearly day-long incarceration in the interior of the glacier plain to see.

The nearly two-hour pull from the icy-cold interior of the crevasse had brought him from unconsciousness through to the realisation that if he were to get out alive, he had to make a supreme effort to help himself. Now that he had nearly attained the surface, he pushed his gloved hands upward to grasp the lip. Mike hunched forward to grasp Tink's anorak as he shouted, 'Get the bloody dogs to do the final pull and we'll have him out.'

A shout from the base commander and the sledge jerked forward. The rope from around Tink's waist jerked loose and flew through the icy gouge, bringing with it Tink's trouser belt, which had snapped at the buckle. Tink desperately tried to get a grip on the icy lip but, with a groan, started to slide back down the crevasse, tearing his anorak out of Mike's clutching hands. With a scream, he fell again into the depths of the crevasse. This time there was no stopping him at the snow wedge, where he had lain so long; he went straight down into the dark depths of the glacier.

~~~

158

The loss of two members of the base within a couple of months had a devastating impact on the surviving members at Admiralty Bay. As it was winter, no external rescue of the remaining members could be attempted until the following spring. One of those who over-wintered there subsequently told me that he was still having nightmares about it, fifty years later. The remaining members had to survive the winter and struggle to cope with their grief until the relief ship, the RRS *John Biscoe*, arrived the following November.

Those of us wintering at the other bases were on tenterhooks all winter, expecting to hear of further deaths at Admiralty Bay. Fortunately no such events took place and a collective sigh of relief went up from all who were overwintering at the British bases. When it was announced in November that the ship had arrived at Admiralty Bay to take everyone off, the news was met with a sigh of relief. The base was closed down, never to reopen under British management. It is now a Brazilian base, with staff and tourists flying from Patagonia.

~~~

In 2000 I went back to Antarctica, to fall for its attractions once again, to refresh the long-faded images, to renew the emotions that still lingered in the recesses of my mind, suppressed but not forgotten. I wanted to visit Admiralty Bay on King George Island where Alan and Tink had died, but I couldn't get there even though I had a half promise we would try when I signed up for the cruise, which was organised by ex-Fids for ex-Fids.

We were heading for Hope Bay, another continental contact, where several members of the cruise had wintered. Deception Island, our last landing, was a day away, so we stopped on the south coast of Livingston and all were allowed to wander the volcanic beach beneath the edge of the ice cap that Alan, Pete and I had traversed so many years ago. I had been on this beach forty-two years earlier, almost to the day. That memory gave rise to all sorts of emotions.

I had not thought of Alan since I'd returned to the UK and visited his parents in Bedfordshire. That had been an awkward visit for me. What does a young man say to bereaved parents? I'd fumbled through, the very fact that I had travelled the fifty or so miles an expression of my regard and friendship for my dead friend.

When I got back on the cruise ship, and after the usual afternoon tea and muffins – so British – I went up to the library forward of the main lounge, for some peace and to read a bit. Quite by chance, I chose a book called *The Crystal Desert* by an American biologist who had worked on the peninsula and who had written this superb evocation of the region and its biology.

I started reading. On page fourteen, he described landing in Admiralty Bay and walking up to two neglected graves, which were side by side near the formerly occupied British base. After wiping them down, he tried to read the names. One was Alan's; the other was that of Tink. As I read their names, I had a most unexpected surge of emotion. For a long moment, I couldn't read. I gazed back at the page. The details of their deaths in print stopped me in my tracks. I put the book down and picked it up again, not once but three times. But I couldn't continue. I put it back on the shelf.

One of the first things I did when I got home was to acquire a copy of the book. But despite repeated efforts I could not get past page fourteen. Only very recently have I been able to read the rest of this excellent book. It still surprises me that I had such an emotional and unexpected return to my youth. I have yet to see Alan and Tink's graves, but I will someday.

A Winter Jolly

Winter was fast approaching. Temperatures were staying below zero for much of the day. Outside the door, the sea in Borge Bay on Signy Island in the South Orkneys was starting to film over into a thin layer of sea ice. Having arrived in late April 1959, I would be in situ for a full year as the resident biologist. My first ice flowers weren't daisies, chrysanthemums or buttercups. They were living in the sea ice cracks. These were a mosaic of interesting ridges where the translucent film of liquid ice had started to break up into separate circular pans of ice. At the edge of the beach next to the jetty, there was an accumulation of these ice flowers. Every little wave thrown up on the beach instantly froze solid, providing the raw material for the developing crystal forest.

It seemed a crime to walk through this field of flowers, leaving footprints crushed into the ice record to be instantly consolidated and blended into a raised beachline of ice of prehistoric proportions. One felt like early man in East Africa, leaving behind, at first, a straight line; then a wandering of footsteps as hesitation set in as the distance from the temporarily sound ice formation closer to shore increased, and the resonance of one's weight rippled outwards across the still-flexible sheet covering the fragile calm of the bay.

When I first saw them, on Borge Bay, I dropped to my knees on the ice-covered beach. Their first blooming was where the calm sea ripples had come ashore and solidified. Sprouting in the frigid -10° water-laden air from every crack were these delicate, fragile, transparent, hexagonal crystals of ice, growing upwards and branching sideways in front of my eyes, as if by magic. Evolving and dissolving with every pulse of the tide.

At first, half an inch, then one, then two, and even three inches high or long, standing rigid until some unseen force caused them to fade away, and an instant later surge up alongside where the conditions were right. As the onset of winter deepened, and when the weather allowed, I would, in the early morning, descend to the beach to see this festival of flowers coming and going.

Later in the winter, when I first went camping, I woke up surrounded by ice crystals, which was puzzling until I realised my breath was providing the necessary moisture. Of course, when I turned the Primus on to heat a cup of iced water into tea, I was showered with a layer of crystals that had built up on the inside of the roof of the tent. These promptly melted, wetting the sleeping bags, and turned back to ice once the Primus was switched off. The following night, the sleeping bags would have to be hung in the apex of the tent to dry out until we wanted to sleep. The Primus heater would have to be turned off, at which point the cycle began again.

While this was annoying, what happened on the walls of the tent was more intriguing and much more fun. As soon as we occupied the inner pyramid of the seven-foot-high tent and the moisture level built up, layer upon layer of crystals grew out from the walls, starting at the floor and climbing up. But the Primus heat changed the dynamics of ice crystal build-up. When the knob was turned and the heat output increased, the layer of crystals would retreat down the walls. As soon as the heat was turned down, they reappeared, growing exponentially up the walls.

When I discovered how to do this, at the turn of my thumb, I got endless fun seeing the growing crystals continuing up or down the walls. There was little else to amuse one in a tent in the Antarctic, in the middle of winter. However, this caper soon got on the wick of my companion and I was told I could only do it when he was outside taking care of the dogs, or for other purposes. Even now, many Antarctic winters later, I can vividly see those hexagonal crystals growing in front of my eyes, like magic.

~~~

Where could I go from Signy to get away from my companions during this long and bitter winter? I racked my brain turning over ideas, one more outlandish than the next. I even started to wake up before breakfast was announced – an unheard-of thing for me. Most, if not all, the ideas flashed across my subconscious in a millisecond, leaving little or no trace. No, I couldn't do a solo traverse of Coronation along its spine, west to east. That would require several teams of huskies (we only had one) and men, most of whom would not go outside the door in the declining autumn and approaching winter. And none with me – the bloody crazy, rash, reckless, bog-trotting Irishman!

No point going there. It would have to be a solo, or near solo, jolly. I talked to Jim, the base leader, and told him I was getting stir-crazy being stuck indoors and having to socialise with a crowd of demented Brits. He said he would ask around. I couldn't go out alone. Was there anyone who would put his life on the line and go with me? I had to come up with a feasible plan. I needed to get away from feeling enclosed and smothered in our base hut. My plan didn't have to be in the official programme. Would 'a winter jolly' be approved? One thing I had learnt in my short sojourn in the bureaucratic jungle of Whitehall, the government HQ, was to never ask a question that you didn't already know the answer to. This plan, whatever it turned out to be, would be sub rosa. The fewer who knew of it, the better. And that included Jim, the official voice of FIDS on base.

It being autumn, I had little outdoor work to do. Virtually all the penguins and birds had taken off to the north to warmer climates. All our resident

163

Paddies, who mutt-mutted the days away, were perched on the kitchen window ledge or, when that was snowed in, on top of the snow pile and as close as possible to the frissons of heat and smells that emanated from there.

Much to my surprise, these Sheathbills stayed the winter long, surviving on scraps that we threw out for them, or tackling the frozen pile of our garbage that developed on the sea ice, in the centre of Borge Bay, which we presumed would go to the bottom after the ice broke up, and to hell with the environment. So birdwatching was out. All that was left was the met observations, which had to be done 24/7 come hail or shine. Ron, the radio operator, sent those to FIDS six times a day and night, for onward transmission to the international met service somewhere like Geneva.

I had just finished reading Shackleton's *South* for the umpteenth time when I wandered into the library to check if there was anything I had not read on the two shelves. William Speirs Bruce's book caught my eye. He was the first Brit – a Scot – to propose a scientific expedition to the Antarctic. He had already been down south in the 1880s and expected to be the leader. However, he was stymied by Clements Markham, president of the Royal Geographical Society, who fancied a young Royal Navy lieutenant named Robert Falcon Scott for the job. Bruce had to settle for leading the first, and only, Scottish National Antarctic Expedition, in 1901–4.

Having landed on the continent and named Coats Land after one of his sponsors, he retired to the South Orkney Islands and set up a base on Laurie Island. There he started the first met programme in the Antarctic. When he left in 1904, having failed to get Britain to take over the station on Laurie and the programme he had started, he offered it to Argentina. They took it over in 1904 and have been running it ever since.

Bingo! Orwell House on Laurie Island was only down the road from

Signy and, more importantly, no one from Signy had ever travelled there in winter. Some poor Brits had tried to get there in summer in a small boat, when they had to be rescued by the Argentines! Which left much egg on HMG's face.

Not wanting a repeat of that, I thought: what if I proposed a winter jolly along the south of Coronation and we just happened to cross the Lewthwaite Strait to Powell Island, where I had spent my first few weeks in Antarctica in December 1957? It would be a courtesy to call into the Argentinians living in Bruce's Orwell House and have a few of the giant T-bone steaks for which Argentina was famous. My companion, whoever he should be, could wet his whistle by supping on a Malbec or two. I, of course, still didn't drink alcohol, which made me even more of an oddball to my Brit companions.

I didn't want this plan to trickle back to FIDS in Stanley for fear of it being banned, so I suggested a trip to check out the seals on the ice along the south coast of Coronation. Karl, our gash hand, who had wintered at Stonington and driven dogs all over, and who was also going stir-crazy, said he might consider coming along provided we didn't do any sledging when the temp got below -10°.

He had gone through the sea ice the previous winter and had barely survived.

We came to that agreement without me mentioning the visit to the Argentine base. The possibility of spending the rest of the winter there with wine and song and steak was thrilling to me. So I approached Jim and announced my wish to do some original research on the seals on the sea ice in winter in the Scotia Sea, adding that Karl was prepared to come and mind me. Jim hummed and hawed, said he would have to consult FIDS in Port Stanley, and went off to compose his message. Later in the afternoon, Ron tapped his nose, indicating that the message had gone. Within twenty-four hours a reply came back. Yes, I could go provided Karl came with me too. The winter jolly was on!

Now that I had the go-ahead, all the planning for the few days in the field had to begin. I had no experience of organising, or leading, such an outing. Nor had anyone on the base, but Karl had participated in several such trips the previous winter down south. I didn't know him very well. He had been a squaddie in the Royal Navy, having stayed on for a three-year tour after his national service. He didn't have much to say during mealtime, surrounded as he was by all these third-level graduates and skilled tradesmen, all of whom had an opinion on everything and weren't shy about giving them.

He came from a working-class background, like George, with whom he tended to be most comfortable. He was quiet and his service in the armed forces would mean that he was used to taking orders, even from a bog-trotter like me. Anyway, we were only going to look at the seals and spend a few nights in a tent on the sea ice within sight of Signy. What could go possibly go wrong?

Planning began. One or two pyramid tents? One for an emergency, or two if we didn't get on and Karl felt like killing me. But there was no question of having two fully loaded tents with duplicate cooking gear as that would make extra weight for the huskies to pull. And they were going to have enough trouble with ten days of food boxes for us and virtually an equal amount of meat bars for the seven dogs.

Perhaps a rifle was required in case we ran out of food? No, the conditions we were going to meet – the hummocks of pack and sea ice that I could see with my binoculars and telescope from Hut Point – suggested we wouldn't get near enough to the seal to shoot it. And there was no guarantee that I would even hit a seal in the conditions of blowing drift that was a constant. So, no lethal weapons. But maybe we might meet a polar bear? I know they have only been found in the Arctic, but you never knew. We were proposing to go to an area never before reached, so anything could happen.

We scrounged around for extra winter gear lest one of us went through the ice and ended in the water, as had happened to Karl the previous winter. But extra skis might be worth their weight in gold if we lost or broke the regular ones. We gradually piled up supplies and camping gear in the jenny shed, and gave the Nansen sled a thorough overhaul, checking all the rawhide lashings holding it together and replacing those that were frayed or looked dodgy. These allowed the sledge to flex, vital in travelling over uneven ice. It was a critical exercise.

We discussed the route we might take. Bernard asked if we were going to circle Signy. Needless to say, I gave that short shrift in view of my hidden objective of spending the rest of the winter as far away from these Brits as I could get. Karl didn't know it, but we were going to be in the lap of luxury, steaks every day and unlimited amounts of Argentinian wine. I salivated at the thought.

We were likely to find the highest number of seals up against the coast of Coronation Island lying out alongside the tidal cracks in the sea ice. We would proceed east along the coast and turn back whenever we'd seen enough seals, if any, or ran out of steam and wanted to get back to a hot bath. No one demurred. After all, I was the seal biologist.

~~~

All the work and activity loading the sledge next to the jetty and laying out the traces caused increased uproar among the dogs. They knew something was happening and hoped they would be involved.

167

The day came. The weather was ideal: blue sky and only a zephyr of wind, which scattered the snow drift across the surface, but not enough to hide its contours. Karl and I were up at the crack of dawn. The early start meant we breakfasted virtually in the dark; it was only a couple of weeks since midwinter's day – the darkest day of the year. We hoped to get away by ten, when dusk would be giving way to the feeble dawn. We left the hut all geared up to go, with our winter windproofs on, from head to toe. All hell broke loose as we approached the span. Every dog leapt to its feet, barking and howling. I went up to Millie, the lead dog of the 'Girls', and unclipped her. She was desperate to get loose. Fortunately, I had a firm grip on her collar and was able to put on her sledging harness.

I had a short lead which I clipped to it. Now she struggled to get down the snow slope to where the loaded sledge stood. I clipped her onto the leading trace as far as it would go from the front of the sledge so we could put the other six dogs two by two on the traces. Flora and Shirley came next.

The only dog left on the span was the giant idiot, Garth, who was being left behind. How he didn't break the heavy wire span with his leaping around and throwing his 110 lbs into the air, I don't know. But the wire span held and before we left he was forced to lie down, exhausted and frustrated.

Once all the dogs were linked to their traces and worn out from straining to get on with the job, Jim ran out to Millie and released the pegged trace. With Karl and I shouting 'Auck!' in unison, she took off, as they all did, straining to pull the frozen-in sledge out of the ice. Karl and several of the base members put their shoulders to the handlebars and rocked the sledge loose. The dogs strained and surged away. Karl grabbed the handlebars and jumped onto the brake pedals at the back, while I with my skis on, grabbed a line attached to the handlebars and survived the sudden lurch of the sledge as it broke out from the frozen ice and snow. We were off!

The sea ice in Borge Bay was lumpy but the dogs and the sledge took it in their stride. Now we were going fast. Within three or four minutes, we had left the bay and were heading out into the Sound and onto the jumbled floes of ice mixed in with iceberg bits and rafts of ten-feet-high slabs of ancient pack ice. After that exhilarating start, once in the hummocky ice, we had to slow, and that's where the skill and experience of the driver came in.

Karl called 'Right!' or 'Left!' and the team, after some confusion, responded to the cracks of the whip. The whip was a strip of rawhide, eight to ten feet long, bound to a foot-long handle made of wood covered with rawhide. It had a loop that the driver put his gloved hand into to prevent him from dropping it, or he hung it on a hook on the handlebars for instant use when needed. I could never get a crack out of the whip, but Karl was an expert. He could crack the whip over the head of an errant dog or two, or even give a painful slap to a particular dog, which brought it back in line. We hadn't got a hundred yards into the hummocky ice when I fell over and saw the 'Girls' and Karl disappear around the nearest berg. I heard various shouts of 'Stop! Stop!' – which obviously stopped me.

A few minutes later, Karl's head appeared above a hummock. 'Are you alright?' he asked. It seemed I was the cause of more slowdowns than the dogs. 'No,' I replied, 'I'm bloody well not.' I tried to disentangle myself from the skis and stand up. 'But I will be in a minute, I hope.' With my skis off, I could stand up. 'Sorry,' I said, sheepishly. What a hopeless git I was. I got back onto the skis and with an 'Auck!' from Karl we were off again.

By the time we were halfway across the Sound, I had fallen twice more. I cursed, as I'm sure Karl did, even though I never heard him. That finished me off. Off came the skis and I jumped on the already overloaded sledge.

169

Would the extra weight bring the sledge to a grinding halt? No, it wouldn't! Millie and the other 'Girls' were up for it, and once the sledge was moving and I was on board, clinging desperately to the tent covering, the dogs hardly paused as they followed their leader through the fresh white snow.

Within a couple of hours, we were close to Coronation and the Laws Glacier with its impressive half-mile-long front and a slew of small and large icebergs being calved continuously, day and night. All they were waiting for was the break-up of the rock-solid sea ice in spring, when they would be spewed into the Sound.

Karl proposed that we make land to set up our first camp. It was a good idea, but I overruled him. I wanted to swing right and head along the coast as far as possible. We had gone less than half a mile when it became obvious that, with the fading light, we'd better get the tent up tout de suite. Karl shouted 'Stop!' into the still air and the 'Girls', as one, stopped, flopped down and lay panting in the snow.

I jumped off the sledge and grabbed my ice axe and the stake needed to peg out team leader Millie and the rest of the dogs. I got hold of Millie's harness and, pulling and stretching out the trace, I pinned it down, hammering the peg into the icy snow layer using the ice axe. Millie dropped down again in exhaustion. Now that the trace was taut, it kept the dogs two by two and reduced the possibility of conflict, always a near-certainty when huskies are allowed to crowd together.

But they weren't the only ones knackered. I certainly was, and Karl looked done in from driving the sledge for nearly six hours, although he wouldn't admit it. We felt we needed to get the pyramid up two-six: in other words, fast.

I unlashed the sledge and turfed the tent on the ground. I picked the only bit of level ground and hurriedly erected the tent. Once we had shovelled snow and ice onto the foot-wide flap, which extended right around the four sides, I crawled into the inner section to spread the four poles and take in the survival gear – sleeping bags and sheepskins to reduce the heat loss to the underlying snow and the snow melt that hot bodies would cause when we rested. Then came a food box and a box containing the Primus and the aluminium pots, pans and plates.

Once the inner tent was organised, I joined Karl outside to help feed the dogs their pound-and-a-half meat bar – all they would get in twenty-four hours. For their water they had to eat the snow. Once that was done, they settled down to sleep, developing a snowy blanket from the drift that had sprung up. By the morning, only their noses would be showing.

When I looked out of the tent that first morning, I got a shock. There was no sign of the huskies. I burst out of the tent and looked around. Thank God! The seven snow-covered bumps had to be the dogs. I approached the one I thought should be Millie and, sure enough, a little of her grey-black muzzle was showing. I reached out to pat it to be met by her white-shrouded body springing up and confronting me. I jumped back. She shook herself, showering me with snow. I got close and grabbed her ears and patted her head, as I did every day at base. She responded, wagging her whole body. We were pleased to see each other. By that time all the other dogs had emerged from their snowy beds, I got back into the tent to wake the snoring Karl.

The sooner we got away, the better. The weather seemed to be holding up. This would be our first full day in the field. We had done nearly ten miles yesterday. I wondered how much time it would take to get to the east end of Coronation – our first objective. Karl prepared breakfast – porridge and dried milk powder with masses of sugar and lumps of butter – in these freezing temperatures we couldn't get enough of it. In fact, on our final night, I put all our remaining butter in the pot with the meat bar and had an inch of melting butter floating on top. We devoured it.

I headed out to climb the highest ice hummock to try to get a perspective on what lay ahead. When I went outside before, I had merely put on my windproof anorak and trousers and no gloves. By the time I re-entered the tent, my fingers and hands were bitterly cold, and my cheeks – ones exposed – were showing signs of frost nip. This time I wore three layers of gloves: a clinging pair of silk gloves, a pair of duffel liners and finally a pair of flexible leather skiing mitts. Now, armed with my trusty ice axe, I was ready to go.

I scrambled to the top of the nearest ice hummock. Steadying myself, I pulled off my two outer fingerless mitts and grabbed the binoculars nestling warmly on my chest beneath the anorak and jumper. I gazed east. I was met with an awe-inspiring dense array of ice pinnacles. Where was the mostly flat sea ice of yesterday? I wondered. This was solid pack ice, probably years old, which had been floating around the islands of the South Orkneys for aeons. What was I letting us in for?

Should we head back? No bloody way. This was my one and only chance to get my name on the map or, if not, at least into the history books.

Push on, never give up! Not at the first hurdle, anyway. I climbed down and re-entered the tent, but not before greeting each and every one of the Girls, who, by then, were all up and eager to go. I put on my brightest possible face and told Karl that it was a grand day and that the temperature was about 2° or 3°. I had hung the thermometer on one of the tent's guy ropes.

In fact, the temperature I recorded was 3°F; in other words, twenty-nine degrees of frost! But I didn't tell Karl that, as he had stipulated before we left that if the temperature went to -5° he would not get out of bed, and he meant it. So I made sure I was out first to take the morning temperature which, with a little adjustment, rarely if ever crossed that barrier.

Once the Nansen was loaded up and all the dogs' harnesses checked, just to make sure they hadn't been chewed during the night, we set off. With the really bad conditions of snow and ice and the tortuous route we had to take, it was a godsend that, having abandoned the skis, more or less, I could jump off the sledge and add my shoulder to the wheel when we got stuck on a bump or a particularly high wave of sastrugi. I was going to get a hell of a lot of opportunity on this trip.

The next day we were changing places on a regular basis. When I took over from Karl for the first time, I got such a surge of adrenaline it nearly blew me away. At last, I was doing what I'd come down south to do – exploring! I was driving a team of huskies into unknown territory, never before touched by man or beast. For a while I was lightheaded, shouting 'Auck!' at the top of my voice until, in my enthusiasm, I nearly turned over the sledge when we hit the next set of frozen waves of sastrugi. That severe wobble brought me back down to earth and the reality that driving a fully loaded sledge over and between a maelstrom of jumbled ice required constant attention and rapid decisions to keep the sledge upright and travelling forward.

It soon became a continuous slog, and it was a great relief when Karl offered to take over. I went back to riding on the sledge or skiing, depending on the conditions. This was a tortuous day, to say the least, as we continually tried to go around all the hummocks, bergy bits and icebergs in our way. Twice we had to go over rather than around. The first time, the 'Girls'

173

manfully pulled us up a sloping shelf of ice, only for the sledge to tip over on its side very near the top. It stopped there, not sliding down, which would have ended our jolly. But we had to unload the sledge and then bring it and the dogs over to the downward slope, man-haul and reload the gear and start again.

The second time we got stuck, we had learnt our lesson – stop while you are ahead. We unloaded much of the gear, drove the team to the other side of the icy slope, unloaded the sledge, drove back over the hummock, reloaded the gear, turned around and retraced our steps, and multiple paw marks, till we got to the deposited gear and supplies, loaded up again, and went our merry way.

We camped soon after that episode. We fed the dogs, crawled into the tent and, after a cup of tea, did an estimate of how far we had travelled. I was shocked. We had gone less than five miles and had been out seven hours! I was despondent and just crawled into my sleeping bag and passed out. That night I had a nightmare. The pack ice we were on had broken up and we were floating past Signy. Next stop was the Weddell Sea. I was glad to wake up in the morning and find we hadn't moved an inch.

Karl and I discussed our position and decided we should try to hug the coast, where we might find some fast ice (frozen sea ice still attached to the land), which should be easier going. That day was better. We found that the pack ice had not penetrated to the coast and, still weaving and bobbing, we made nearly ten miles. I had been hoping to get to the east end of Coronation in three or four days, but it was probably going to take us seven-plus days. Ten days was the max; we would have to turn back at that point to ensure we had enough food for man and beast on the return journey.

Of course, if we made it to Laurie Island and the Argentinians, it wouldn't matter. All this depended on the weather. If we got a severe blow that night it would force us to stay put for several days and that would be a disaster. We hadn't yet seen sight or sound of a seal, so the trip would be classed as a failure. But maybe if and when we got to the Lewthwaite Strait we might find a few.

By day six, we were three-quarter ways down the coast. The routine for us and the 'Girls' was established. Things were in our favour: each day we got up, it was a little lighter and brighter. The lengthening days lifted our spirits. Day seven turned out to be exciting. I saw a black object on the ice in the distance and called a halt. The trusty binoculars came from their warm abode. I focused. It was a penguin! A tall, statuesque Emperor penguin! What in God's name was it doing out here on the ice 1,000 or 2,000 miles from the nearest rookery?

All the South Orkney Islands were surrounded by fast ice, probably extending for hundreds of miles. Did it walk from its breeding rookery at Halley Bay coast, a mere 1,900 miles away?

However it got here, it was standing upright and looked bemused (if a penguin can look bemused). What to do? Photograph it? Shoot it? After all, we had never seen an Emperor penguin in the South Orkneys before. But before I could even think of pulling out the rifle, the Emperor moved, the dogs pricked up their ears, and Millie started howling.

I was standing beside the sledge discussing our next move when all the 'Girls' joined in. With a sudden lurch, the sledge broke out of the ice and started moving. Karl, standing on the brakes and holding onto the handlebars, was caught napping by the lurch and was thrown to one side. As the sledge picked up speed, I desperately flung myself at it as it surged past, grabbing the handlebars and shouting 'Stop!' repeatedly at the top of my voice. By now, all the 'Girls' were in full voice and rushing to get to the penguin and have their first real meal in over a week. What to do? I clung on desperately. It was obvious that they would stop at nothing to get the prize. We thundered across a few waves of sastrugi. As we started across the next one, with the front of the sledge suspended in the air, I threw all my weight to the right side, lifting the now airborne sledge onto its right runner. The sledge tottered in mid-air and then added its weight to the turning-over movement. Initially, it was on its side and ploughing a groove in the snow and ice surface. The dogs were all jerked to a halt, their howls muted in frustration at seeing their next meal flop onto its belly and, paddling furiously, disappear among the icy ridges.

I picked myself up, rushed forward with the rope's end in my stronger left hand and took out my frustration by whacking each dog on the head or body, whichever was handiest, as I passed, until I got to Winnie, standing up defiantly. By that time, I had run out of frustration and puff. I could only fling myself at her, bowling her over and sprawling on top of her heaving body. With Winnie down, the rest of the dogs quietened down. Karl, who had recovered, ran forward and helped me get off Winnie before pegging her out. The Emperor was nowhere to be seen.

Once we had unloaded the sledge, put it back on its runners and reloaded, it was time to take a tea break. That meant me taking the equipment box off the sledge – again – and getting out the Primus while Karl built a snow wall to protect us, and it, from the wafting drift and freezing breeze. Soon I had melted enough snow in the teapot and we were savouring a life-reviving brew. It was one of those timeless moments. Despite the near disaster, or maybe because of it, we were relaxing, our backs to the wind as we gazed out at the magnificent ice ramparts of the coast of Coronation Island.

Today we would reach the Lewthwaite Strait separating Coronation Island from Powell, where I had spent my first day in the Antarctic; sure wasn't that the Pinnacle Rocks off St Michael's Island at the entrance to it right in our faces, and less than ten miles away? I had no doubt that we would be camping east of them tonight. Restored by the brew, we hurried to get going again. The dogs were up for it and so were we. And the going was getting easier; more sea ice and marginally fewer hummocks and berg bits. By midday, we were passing the Pinnacle Rocks. Before us was the Lewthwaite and beyond that the outline of Powell Island and the western end of Laurie Island. We were on the brink of success.

I smiled. Should I tell Karl my plan to winter with the Argentinians? It was consuming me. How had I kept it secret all these days and nights, especially in the tent where we had discussed every aspect of the trip, specifically how we were going to get home to Signy?

The 'Girls' pushed on, picking up their pace. The snow and sea ice was much flatter here. Maybe it had broken up and reformed recently. After another few hundred yards, the sea ice became completely smooth and had a translucent bluish-green colour. It was virtually bare of snow cover. I called a halt. Everywhere, as far as we could see, the sea ice seemed to be the same: translucent but firm. There was no trouble carrying our weight.

I took out my trusty ice axe and started chopping and chipping a hole. I penetrated through to the sea. We estimated its thickness – eight inches! Obviously, this was new sea ice. How long had it been there? A week, a day, overnight? We had almost ten miles to go before we would be safe on Powell. The dogs would be happy to try, but the question was whether we should take the chance. I recalled the Dion Island tragedy the previous winter, when three Fids had camped on the sea ice and it had blown out under them, drowning all three. Amazingly, most of their dogs survived.

Karl was for turning back instantly. I was all for discussing if we should head for Michael's Pinnacle and camp to see what the morning would bring. 'No,' said Karl, 'let's head back.' I put up my binoculars. Powell, with its vague shape of Laurie behind, was tantalisingly close. That vision remains with me as if it were yesterday. I nodded to Karl. 'OK. Let's go home.'

We turned the 'Girls' and headed west of Michael's Pinnacle. We had another week of hard slogging until the ice cap of Signy appeared over the horizon. Once we entered Borge Bay and the base hut appeared, the Girls, dog-tired as they were, picked up their paws and raced home. They, and we, were pleased to have survived the winter jolly. We had been out more than two weeks and had not seen a single seal, but the Emperor nearly made up for it. Nor had we got to Laurie and the T-bone steaks and wine. We were back where we started, with none of our objectives realised.

Was it all a miserable failure? When I recovered from the last day's frantic rush across the Sound to Borge Bay and the welcoming lights of Tonsberg House, I realised that the winter jolly had been a success. This was the first time anyone had ever sledged along the Coronation coast to the Lewthwaite Strait. We had done close to two hundred miles, if you took all the turns and twists into account. And I had learnt how not to drive a sledge with Winnie and the rest of the boisterous team of Girls. I was fit like never before, and Karl and I hadn't killed each other. In fact, we ended up being very comfortable with one another, which was the major achievement.

Frozen Seas

I had never before seen the sea freeze, and for those of us not living in the frozen north it is a revelation. If I'd thought about it at all, I thought it probably happened overnight. You'd go to bed on a calm night and wake up to find the sea outside the door frozen, at least in our sheltered Borge Bay. By the time I was dumped at Signy, in April, the temperature had started to drop, with really chilly evenings occasionally down to 15° or 10°F (-10°C). Even on calm nights there was no sign of a freeze-up. I used to go out first thing in the morning in the hope that something had happened and that I would see it before the sun or wind got up and it melted and disappeared. But there was never a bit of it.

It became a standing joke: would I, by staring intently at the sea in the early morning, cause it to freeze up before my eyes, and thus fuck up the last-minute rush to collect seals to feed the dogs (and an occasional human) during the long winter months? Once the freeze arrived, small boating with a two-and-a-half horsepower Seagull outboard engine would be impossible, even in the early stages.

It wasn't until two or three days of calm at the start of May that the first real signs appeared. The initial sign was new ice forming on the beach. In the mornings, the rocks and beach pebbles at the edge were slippery with a film of clear, transparent ice. I started to lose interest in skimming, my early morning alternative to calisthenics. On calm mornings, I had found that hunting flat stones that skipped two or three or even five or six times across the incoming sea was mentally and physically satisfying.

However, with the temperature down and the early-morning ice layer, the usual ten or fifteen minutes' warm-up soon resulted in freezing fingers and aching knuckles. The longer I went on, the more frost-nipped palms discouraged this harmless recreation. Soon, if it was calm, I was out kicking the stones instead, to see if the freezing was tough enough to prevent them being kicked into the sea.

Within a few days, there was a crusty layer of white, salty ice consolidating the beach edge, and a thin layer of clear ice extending a few inches out. With the departure of the tide, the ice snapped off under its own weight. After a couple of days of low temperatures, this edge thickened and survived. After clearing the snow or ice crystals from my favourite beach boulder, I would sit quietly watching the early morning sun glinting and gleaming off this intricate network of ice, snow and sea, though I didn't stay long enough for frost nip to set in.

An oily looking skim over the surface appeared, glistening in the sunlight and sparkling as the swells caressed its underside in passing. This was interspersed with small crystal nodules, accretions of ice crystals, which formed when the oily sheet was dispersed by waves or even relatively small ripples. Over a week or ten days, it formed and reformed until it seemed that the bergy bits were caught in an icy gruel, an ever-thickening porridge of sea ice from which they were unable to break free.

We now had a mush of sea-ice crystals, all trying to cling to one another and being torn apart by the daily cycle of lunar gravity, forcing the tide to withdraw its support, or by any wind in excess of a few miles an hour, forcing the kernels of ice crystals to push up against one another and even try to climb over their downtrodden siblings. Soon, plate-sized pancakes of sea ice started to appear with turned-up edges where they banged up against their neighbour. When such ice pancakes appeared, they were piled up on the beach edge, thickening the existing layers and forming a rampart that the waves banged up against and spilled over, leaving puddles on the inside that

180

soon froze solid among the rocks and boulders.

One morning I came out to a blue sky, high alto-cirrus, probably 20,000 feet up, a very gentle breeze that flushed the exposed cheeks, and a hazy sun surrounded by a halo of something – ice crystals? When I looked at Borge Bay my heart leapt. Wow! It has happened, I thought. Right across the bay, the oily sheet was now complete and the rippling waves were no longer breaking it up.

I walked down to the jetty and, lying at full stretch, reached down and plunged my hand into the sheet to pluck a piece. On inspection, it looked just like the mushy sea ice I'd been seeing for days, but the difference was that the upper surface now had a hard, shiny layer of protruding ice crystals. Now sufficiently thick, it was able to withstand the wave action and by its very weight was damping down the sea.

'Looks like we'll be walking on the sea ice shortly,' I said at breakfast. I smiled at the assembled mob, my excitement palpable. 'Rather you than me,' replied George. 'But why are you waiting?' he continued, an evil grin gleaming from his dark-brown eyes. 'One bogman less, more grub and booze for us.' 'Maybe Bernard should try, he's the lightest of us all,' I replied. Bernard looked shocked, his quiet soul leaping at the thought of taking the lead in a dangerous enterprise. 'Hold your horses, it'll be another few days before that is on,' Jim said, the auld hand of experience showing.

After breakfast, we all went out to have a look. Only an emergency, such as the hut going on fire or some such disaster, would take people away from breakfast. By now, with the temperature well below zero, my breath was freezing as it came out, the moisture in it crystallising instantly, clinging to my beard, forming an icy layer. The air trapped inside provided a cushion, preventing the skin on my chin from freezing. It was the only reason I tolerated the beard. It was continually irritating; in fact, it was a bloody nuisance. It was itchy and filled with various objects – from crumbs to soup and mouldering proteins such as bright orange or pink penguin egg yolk, or pieces of seal, penguin or other sundry birds' meat and feathers, and the all-pervading oil, grease and gunk remaining from dissections and activities such as feeding seals to dogs. It always amazed me how much hair, fur and gristle spattered around when using an axe on the deeply frozen seal carcasses piled up above the tide line below the hut, and used as the winter supply of protein for man and beast.

With the wind chill at a minimum as there was only a gentle zephyr of a breeze blowing, my nether regions were what would determine the length of my contemplation, as my half-empty rucksack – I only carried the minimal survival gear and the tools of the trade, my binoculars, which were hanging around my neck – would have provided a less than adequate cushion and would, if used, be penetrated by the ambient temperature in not more than five minutes.

So, contemplation was not a protracted affair but rather a moveable feast. But that day I seemed to have stayed still forever. Or was it only a short period between my strenuous climb uphill and the rapid seeping away of that life-sustaining body heat?

But this was too much mental gymnastics for my freezing nether regions. And my brain, unaccustomed as it was to anything deeper than *Where is that fucking thing?* whatever it was I was looking for at the time. I pulled the fur-trimmed anorak hood tight around my face, gripped the long ski poles, and pushed off home. Back to the reality of isolation; back to the group, who would make all our survival possible. From now on, through the depths of winter until the late spring, we were totally isolated with no possibility of outside help.

A frozen sea in every direction: south, as you might expect, but now east and west and north as well. Did it just extend as far as the horizon, or to infinity? Or for the length of the Weddell Sea, as far as 2,000 miles away? Or north, surrounding Coronation and Laurie Islands and shrouding the whole South Orkneys with a massive skirt of sea ice? But how far north? One mile? One hundred or more? In the days before satellites, my guess was as good as the next.

I set off down the hill to the hut, to security, to companionship, and to survival.

~~~

Giant Petrels – Stinkers – never appealed to me. As their proper name suggests, they are the biggest members of the Petrel or tubenose family, a group of elegant oceanic aeronauts. The Petrels were nearly as big as their cousins, the Albatross; in fact, they were bigger than some of the smaller species of Albatross. And though they tried to emulate their better-known relations (better known only because of Coleridge and the Ancient Mariner), gliding and swinging on the ocean winds, they would never be as elegant. They had also a less-than-striking plumage, unlike the Albatross, most of which are just beautiful. The Stinkers were mostly mottled browns and greys, with some being white, or nearly so. Their long creamy bill, with nostrils set in two great tubes running down along it (hence the tubenose family name), suggested an ugliness, just as the glint in the small yellow eye suggested a cruel rapaciousness.

On base, I always called them GPs. After all, I was the official birdwatcher, employed as a biologist, and had to show the way, wave the flag, do the right thing. This lasted until I had cause to put leg rings on large numbers of GPs in my last autumn in the Antarctic at Signy Island.

The September after I came back from Antarctica, a mention of GPs at an august discussion at the Zoological Society in London brought the smell back to me; that oily, sticky, gooey white smell of half-digested fish mixed with the blue-black inky smell of squid, added to the pink crab-like smell of the disembowelled krill. There was an instantaneous synaptic connection: my olfactory bulbs flared; the screen in my frontal lobes lit up with a smell of impending doom. I still get it even now – just thinking about it, aeons later and a world apart.

My diary records them as one of the first Antarctic species to greet us on the way, spotted south of the equator, together with the brown-and-white-dappled Cape Pigeon, whose colouring appropriately gave them the name 'pintado' along the South American coast. These beautiful small-pigeon-sized birds were a breath of fresh and cool Antarctic air, drifting north on the scarcely moving wind of the trades; dropping down for a sudden nibble on any scrap thrown overboard.

They scarcely ever left us from then on. No matter the weather – hail, rain or hell's fury – they were to be seen, except during the depth of the Antarctic winter when the only fools to stay, other than ourselves, were the Sheathbills or Paddies.

Once the initial thrill of adding the Stinker to the list of new species seen from the *Shack* had passed, they became part of the background scene, rarely absent, rarely noticed whether on land or at sea in the Southern Ocean. They produce a less than delicate secretion, or 'gurp', as it was known to the intrepid bird-ringers of the Antarctic. This is secreted by the lining of the proventriculus, that part of the bird's gut used for defensive purposes, when it is spat at the adversary. No doubt it also has a digestive function, but no one has, surprisingly, looked for one. It is, as one might imagine, used mainly on the breeding grounds in holding territory against invaders, or driving off avian predators like the voracious skuas, or scavengers such as the Paddies.

All the Petrel family produce it to a lesser or greater extent. Of course, Giant Petrels have it in giant quantities. The pear-shaped young, engorged with fat and unable to move for weeks, were an easy and succulent prey for the protein-starved sealers. The young nearly all had their crops full of fish, krill or squid and, not surprisingly, when approached by a monstrous predator in the form of an evil-smelling, slobbering sealer, they reacted instinctively by producing not merely as much as they had of the equally evil-smelling gurp, but also as much of their last meal as they could spew up.

Often the aiming and timing were good – I can vouch for both – with the result that the sealer got a faceful, before the luckless Stinker chick met its untimely end. Despite their unfortunate nickname and habits, GPs were fascinating members of the Antarctic scene. They were ubiquitous, but with large concentrations in the Antarctic fringe of the South American sector. On Signy we had a population of more than 2,500; we counted 1,241 nests stretching along the rough hillside beneath the ice cap on the west coast.

The GPs were semi-colonial, nesting in relative proximity on an appropriate headland or protuberance from which they could launch their ungainly bodies (ungainly on the ground, that is) into the onshore wind, soaring away after the first few flaps gave them the lift to allow their long wings, built for gliding the ocean's waves, to pick up the aerial currents and glide off downwind like thistledown under full control.

This sense of aerial buoyancy was totally missing on land. Like all Petrels, their legs are set further back than many other birds: with the exception of penguins, of course, whose legs are stuck on at the aft end! As a result, they can only waddle, bouncing their breasts off any bump in the ground, and then resting frequently.

If you disturb them on a calm day, when lift-off requires the proximity of a cliff edge, they rush off with a squawk of alarm, wings half-extended, slipping and banging themselves off every obstacle in their way until they reach a cliff or the safety of the sea, which, on Signy, was rarely more than a couple of hundred yards away. There they would paddle around, eyeing you with mistrust and waiting to return to the large single egg – several times hen's egg size – cooling rapidly in the chilling air.

It is at such times that the opportunist predators such as the skua or Paddy nip in to attack the eggs. Often the shell is too thick even for the savagely hooked bill of the skua. Though only a gull in wolf's clothing, they closely resemble the eagle with their piercing stare, their hooked bill and talons always ready for the fray. After several unsuccessful attempts to pierce the shell, I have seen Paddies push the egg around until it toppled out of the shallow nest, and pursue it downhill until it eventually cracked, revealing the rich red yolk or the half-formed chick, either of which was gulped down with dispatch. All the while they were turning their heads, constantly watching for any competition, or making a quick jab at another skua or a circling Paddy, ever hopeful that something would be left to feed their hungry chicks.

Petrels are good birds to study, aside from the fact that the two sexes look like identical twins. Obligingly, their one large egg makes sexing them easy if you catch them before its arrival. If you succeed in grabbing the bird on the nest, you can feel the egg without any problems, which means that the other bird, which promptly takes over the incubation once the egg is laid, must be the male.

186

Most of these birds had sufficiently different coloured plumages that identification at the nest was easy. Off the nest was another matter, and for that we put on large but light metal bands with a number marked in two places. The bands were overlapped around the bird's 'leg' – it is really its ankle, anatomically speaking. The overlapping metal protected one number from the abrasion of wind, sea and rocks, so that even years later it could be identified if the number on the outside was, by then, an eroded blur. Nowadays, even if the number is totally obliterated, electronic techniques developed by the police for identifying filed-off gun numbers can be used to bring up the number and add it to the scientific record for the benefit of posterity.

In contrast to the Albatross, GPs have poorly developed courtship displays. They engage in some head waving between the pair on the ground and the occasional low-level zoom over the nest site with flaps down and head waving to and fro, but that is about all that they do. However, they make up for all their ungainliness – if not their odiferous habits – by being spectacular migrants. Perhaps 'migrants' is not the right word because that conveys a definite destination; with GPs, there appears to be no such intention but, like so many young people, it seems merely a desire to get away from their place of origin, and travel. And this they do with great abandon.

For the three or four years after they leave the nest as plump ten-pounders, they travel continuously, winging the southern seas on the westerlies from their breeding grounds below South America, bouncing off the Cape of Good Hope (alive mostly), to turn up in Perth or Tasmania or in New Zealand (not always alive), before finally returning – having circled the Antarctic certainly more than once, and probably many times – to their island of origin to breed and continue the circle of life.

The ringing programme on Signy was the first such study. It had gone on for five-plus years and led to this globetrotting picture emerging. Every ring recovered on corpses washed up on beaches, on birds caught in fishing nets, or by colleagues around the southern hemisphere, added another piece to the jigsaw. Finally, four years after the first young chicks were ringed, one numbered GP 13442 – a mottled grey-brown, undistinguished-looking bird – appeared in the western sky. With its hormones bubbling, it landed clumsily on a small ridge on the west coast of Signy. It wasn't long before the annual spring inspection of the nest sites looking for ringed birds revealed its presence.

All those efforts ringing young birds in the cold chill of autumn, stoically turning the other cheek to the Stinkers' revenge, had at last paid off. It was finally proven that GPs do circumnavigate the polar continent and home in on their speck of a home with uncanny accuracy. This was the reward for all that effort: one small cog added to the wheel of knowledge.

Ringing GP chicks was a feature of the biological programme at Signy, as well as regular recording of the presence of ringed adults. The scheme had been begun by Dr Bill Sladen, the well-known biologist, more than a decade before. Lance Tickell, a biologist employed as a met man, had ringed many of the nest-bound chicks in the autumn a couple of years before my arrival. It was not a job the base members relished.

It required several weeks of work in the field, often in deteriorating weather conditions. And there were too many stories of the bird-banders being banished on their return to the emergency hut at Hut Point until the all-pervading smell wore off. Others had been forced to wash, which was regarded in the Antarctic as a fate worse than death!

So when the time came, my call for volunteers fell on deaf ears. That is something of an understatement; in fact, it was my ears that were deafened by the response. I got the impression that there was a definite lack of enthusiasm for this particular aspect of the scientific programme.

Generally, base members were extremely willing to lend a hand for the goriest of dissections, or for uncomfortable assistance beyond the call of duty – all in the cause of science and to reduce the boredom of daily life.

However, this was regarded as being above and beyond the call. All inducements, such as my thousands of cigarettes and pounds of free tobacco, which was the ration I'd accumulated through my abstinence from smoking for more than a year, failed to rouse them. They knew I wouldn't take them home with me anyway. Offers of meals in the Savoy or other such establishments also failed to arouse the response one might otherwise have expected. Cynicism was rife. Pleas that the scientific programme would be seriously damaged met with exclamations of 'FO!': no, not the Foreign Office. In fact, 'SPF' (Shit Pants Fergus) became the mantra, shouted every time I appeared about to raise the issue of the holiday camp on the west coast.

The real issue, that of safety, was merely muttered into the beards of those who were in the last month or six weeks of their sojourn in Antarctica. 'I wouldn't go across the road with that wild reckless bastard' was the sentiment. Everyone, including myself, was increasingly conscious of the fact that their two and a half years in the Antarctic was coming to an end. We had survived; Alan and Tink, along with three others, had not.

In the end I went alone with promises of help, from Jim and Karl, which never materialized, ringing in my ears: chugging away from the jetty, loaded down with tents and the hundreds of rings I imagined I was going to clap on every chick in sight. In a final gesture of friendship, I gave them the time-honoured signal for victory and departed with the clouds gathering darkly in the west.

They had promised faithfully to transport (and rebuild) the whalers' hut close to the base hut that Jim and Bill had pulled down for, they said, my benefit and comfort. It was to be re-erected on the west coast. It was built the following year after my return to civilisation when, ensconced in headquarters in London, I insisted that it be included in the work programme so the Stinker study could continue with at least the minimum of comfort for ringers.

The next volunteer to take on the role of bird ringer on base arrived just after I finished my Stinker season. Roger Filer was fresh out of college and eager to do things. While I was still on base, I taught him how to ring birds. Not Stinkers – they had all fledged – but the adult Storm Petrels that lived under stones around the hut, as well as the collection of Paddies that lived off our leavings. After I left, Roger carried on the study, but died eight months later when he fell off a rock face on Gourlay during a ringing expedition to a Paddy nesting stronghold.

~~~

On my journey out to ring the Giant Petrel chicks on the west coast, the weather looked ominous, and there was a build-up of heavy cumulus. The sun was shining but I was not sure how long for. I was going alone; no one had offered to come with me. Was it because of the risks involved, with repatriation so close? Or was it that spending ten days covered in Giant Petrel vomit and having to put up with that dangerous Irish git was a step too far? Heading across Borge Bay in the twelve-foot fibreglass pram, I was hoping to make it to Signy's west coast and set up camp before the weather deteriorated. I got the tent up but the ground flap was not rock loaded, nor

190

was all the equipment inside, before the first tell-tale splatters of freezing rain arrived. Within minutes I was soaked and frozen. It presaged a couple of weeks of the most uncomfortable camping I ever experienced, then or since.

Having stowed the gear, I settled down to eat the standard camp gruel pemmican with a happy thought for the morrow and the job ahead. Just think of it, all these happy little Stinkers waiting to get a ring clamped on their leg and enter the log book of history. With a warm glow – caused more by the blast of the heater than the meal – I slid down into my Black's double Icelandic sleeping bag, feeling the thickness of beautiful down absorb and reflect back all that body heat, until I was in a cocoon of blissful warmth. One hand reached out to switch off the Primus heater.

With what seemed only a fractional pause, the cold came seeping in. Within a few truncated minutes, the only extremity exposed to the chill – my nose – was touched with frost. The drawstring was pulled that extra bit tighter around my face to ensure that all avenues of access for the cold were cut to a minimum. Tomorrow I would get among the birds. With a relaxed contentment, I closed my eyes. Sleep, as always, was instantaneous.

After nearly two weeks of continuous banding, every catchable Stinker chick was banded and in the GPs' history book. But there was a price to pay. I had also experienced the most unpleasant, uncomfortable, trying and difficult conditions of my whole stay in Antarctica.

That first day, I emerged bright and early. Well, perhaps not so bright and certainly not so early – it being late autumn meant that one could stay snuggled up in the down until 8.30 am or 9 am, as no effective work could begin before the 9 am dawn.

A quick peek outside before the breakfast ritual of thick black tea or chocolate convinced me I was in for a bad day. The sunlight, such as it was, glimmered through a mist of rain. It was coming down in sheets from banks of grey-black cloud, and driven by the prevailing west wind. The thermometer, tied to the tent guy and close to the sleeve, was flying horizontally in the wind. It showed a rise of more than ten degrees from the night before; it was now hovering just around freezing point, between 31°F and 32°F. I knew, even before feeling it, that the rain would be freezing. It was on the brink of being ice but just not making it. I emerged into the worst sort of conditions I could have for the job I was about to begin.

The freezing rain would ensure that I would get soaked through and despite the heavy windproof anorak, trousers, long johns and multiple upper layers, I gradually got more and more chilled as the day wore on. Also, the near-freezing temperature would make the handling of the metal bands hell. Using the metal pliers necessary to clench the ring around the bird's leg would mean frozen fingers and burnt skin; in this case, burnt by the cold of the metal, not the heat. As if this wasn't enough, the extra weight of rain-soaked clothes added to the exhaustion from struggling up and down rock-strewn slopes all day.

I hesitated outside the sleeve entrance of the tent, partly sheltered from the driving, freezing rain. Why not go back in and put one's feet up and wait for better weather? Who the hell would know anyway? So a few bloody Stinkers wouldn't make the record book. Who cares? Not those buggers on base huddled around the Aga, drinking tea and stuffing themselves with Charlie's hot scones.

Unfortunately, my competitive spirit won out. If I didn't start now, I'd never get the whole population done. Daily, birds were fledging and leaving the nest to trundle ungainly to the sea, there to toss around until they slimmed down and their wing muscles could lift them up on the ocean's breath. The number of birds done would be down from last year, and those baskets at base would be saying that I'd spent my time lying in my pit instead of ringing.

I pulled the hood tight around my face and headed down wind to the nearest group of nests, no more than thirty yards away. The young Stinker was huddled on its wet, stony nest, head tucked into its chest, staring balefully out to sea, its yellow iris flickering. The bastard had seen me. I closed in on the chick, rapidly pulling off my mitts and grabbing at its neck. It lumbered upright in the nest, squawking in alarm.

Within the batting of an eyelid, or in this case a nictitating membrane – birds not having eyelids – it had weaved away from my bare clutching left hand and, with perfect politeness, grabbed my outstretched fingers. With a convincing snapping motion, it clamped onto them with its four-inch beak. I yelled. What, I don't remember, but it certainly was not polite. I responded in kind, punching it hard on the side of the head with my right fist. Not unnaturally, it let go of my finger and fell over, looking somewhat dazed. Damn, I could see the blood welling up in the bruise caused by the beak. That would be stiff and sore shortly. Without further ado, I put my knee on its neck, flung myself over its half-extended wings and grabbed its right 'leg'.

By the time I had sorted out the correct ring, and clenched it around its leg below the 'knee', it was back on form, clattering its bill, endeavouring to shake its head, and struggling to flap its wings. I completed the job, making sure the ring was circular and that it moved freely up and down the leg. I took my knee off its neck and jumped up. The chick struggled to get upright and at the same time do its defence mechanism bit.

Fortunately, I had moved upwind of it and its first spew blew back in its own face. This seemed to incense it and it then proceeded to make a supreme effort and succeeded in gurping up most of its last meal of partly digested *Notothenia*, the cod-like fish found plentifully in the coastal zone.

This heap of fishy vomit, which must have weighed a pound and a half, was piled up on the nearby rocks. The bird lumbered off crab-like into the wind using its paddle-like feet for five yards or so before settling down to gabble hysterically at me for a moment, then it stupidly tucked its head back on its shoulders and stared out to sea once again.

I started for the next bird, five or six yards upwind. It had been watching its neighbour struggle with great equanimity, or so it seemed. But as soon as I moved, its neck shot out straight at me and I was greeted with a shower of dark oily green and orange gurp that splattered off my shoulder and down my sleeve and hand. My nostrils were assailed by an incredible pungent smell of rotten fish and cod liver oil. Fifteen feet, with the wind – not bad. Learn the lesson and next time approach downwind.

I rapidly worked out a technique whereby when I approached the nest I waved my left hand in front of and above the chick's head while grabbing its neck with my right hand. This meant that the initial bill lunge and its accompanying spew were directed away from me. Of course, it didn't work all the time and every so often one would get me. As the birds were often on rocky knolls, the approach required climbing uphill. On one such occasion I came up over the edge of a knoll to find a bird staring at me at eye level and within inches of my face.

We were both surprised. I reacted fast – throwing up a hand to cover my eyes, to no avail. The force of his wretched retching was only partly blocked and I received a face full of dripping fish. I struggled to maintain my footing on the rock on which I was balanced precariously. By the time I recovered

194

and wiped my face (with the sleeve of my anorak), the bird had flown.

Fortunately, the full-frontal attack was successful on only one other occasion during the two weeks. One and a half thousand birds later, there had been many near misses, which meant only being covered in the oily fish spray, thus ensuring that I would have attracted every cat within a five-mile radius, if there had been any cats, and repelled everyone else. In fact, I worked out later that fewer than 10 per cent, a mere 150 or so, had got me. It is not hard to imagine the overall effect.

The freezing drizzle never let up for the whole two weeks except for an occasional respite and for a slight warming up in the middle of the day. This was compensated by a corresponding decline below freezing as the day wore on, so that I was permanently soaking wet or freezing wet. Added to that was the fact that as soon as the temperature dropped, my fingers stuck to the ringing pliers.

To bend the ring into shape and clamp it tight around the bird's leg, while hanging on to its neck, required the removal of all the outer gloves. The inner silk ones, which I had used all winter, were torn and ragged and had no finger ends left. By the end of the couple of weeks, all my fingertips had lost skin and several were blistered, making the continuous use of the pliers a painful experience. The medical books, politely, called this frost nip. Frost nip, for God's sake! What I called it in my diary was of such a sulphurous nature that to repeat it here would burn a hole in the page!

Gradually, the rotten fish smell turned into that of rotten eggs but, being in contact with the smell on a twenty-four-hour basis, I was becoming inured to it. However, once back at the tent, I could not bear the stench of having my anorak or trousers inside to dry out and had to leave both between the inner and outer tents, isolating the major source of putridness, more or less.

Because the temperature there was considerably less than inside the inner tent, the smell was less noticeable.

Of course, it meant that my outer clothes never dried out and they froze solid during the lower temperatures at night. Thawing them out in the morning, with the consequent rush of odours of putrefaction, and putting them on wet was a constant source of irritation and meant that every day started off badly. This was not improved by the continually bad weather. On several days, it was just too bad for me to go out. I doubt if I ever wanted any job to finish as much as I did that one of ringing Stinker chicks this time.

Great care is needed when boating in Antarctic waters, whether in a ship or in a dinghy, because bergy bits or 'growlers', as small icebergs are called, with only maybe five or ten feet showing above the surface but with nine-tenths beneath, may not be picked up until too late, as we were to find out to our regret. I always wondered why growlers were so called, because, despite seeing hundreds of them in the years spent south, I never heard anything resembling a growl. Oh yes, lots of bangs, whooshes, plops and even creaks, but never a growl. So I was unprepared for the experience. I had just a few weeks of tent life ahead of me before I departed the Antarctic for home.

This day, 7 April 1960 to be exact, the afternoon sky had brightened and brought with it a calm that transmitted itself to all things. The choppy seas reduced their angry slapping of the shoreline to a quiet murmur. The high level of cirrus, pink-stained with the rays of the departing sun, merely fanned a rustle of wind across one's cheeks. Even the raucous Stinkers gave up their unpredictable gobbling.

For the first time in a week I could sit outside the tent and contemplate nature, letting my imagination run riot over the distant snowy hills that were rosily glowing with gratitude to the sun-giver, and casting my mind's eye south across the ice-strewn Weddell Sea to the continent, at that point 1,800 miles of impassable pack ice away.

I went to bed content and was instantly asleep. Sometime later, I lurched awake. I peered through the gloom of the tent, trying to focus on the cause of my wakefulness, and then I heard it – a long, drawn-out, shuddering groan that filled the tent with air vibrating in sympathy with my sudden attack of nerves. It died away slowly, leaving behind a vacuum of stillness as disturbing as itself.

Hardly had the stillness begun than it was racked by a repeat. This time it seemed that the beast must have arrived right alongside the tent and was breathing his foul-mouthed temper over me. I struggled upright in my bag, pulling and tugging at the tie string that imprisoned my shoulders. A successful pull on the solidified string catapulted me half out and across the tent.

I hurriedly pulled on anorak and trousers, determined not to be had in my bed. While I struggled to dress, the sound seemed to abate. I paused, ears pulled back to catch every nuance. A sibilant hiss dying away was all I caught, as if 'it' had expired, overcome at the thought of having me on the menu. I burst out of the tent, ready to run. There are no large land animals in Antarctica, and even though I was camped a mere ten yards from the shore, I couldn't imagine even a Killer whale making it across the intervening rocky beach. I crouched, head turning to locate the sound, and peered through the gloom.

All was silent: that self-same tangible stillness. But as I listened, reality crept through a crack in my illusion and I could hear the soft lapping of the waves. *Grruuum* ... The growl filled the air again. This time, with my senses at maximum alert, I zoomed in on the site. In the gloom, the gleam of the

197

star-studded sky reflected off the top of a small iceberg, not more than ten feet of it showing. It was wallowing past, about thirty yards out in the current. Carefully balanced, it tipped to and fro with every passing swell, and as it did so some internal stress caused these eerie howls to emerge. I laughed with relief and watched it disappear in the gloom, wallowing and growling, grumbling like a prehistoric monster that had lost its evening meal. Ever since, I have changed my attitude of disdain to one of respect. Growlers how are ye: ruddy great lions, more like. Definitely not to be taken lightly.

Like all things, good and bad, my time ringing GPs came to an end and as soon as I ran out of chicks to ring, I headed for base, leaving all the gear and tents there to be picked up later. I had banded 1,574 chicks over ten days of continual work. Not much per day, you might say: my answer to that is that you should try it sometime!

As I prepared for the return to base, it was raining again but my spirits were lifting by the minute. I even had the energy to set the camera on a rock and take a shot of my bedraggled self for posterity! (see photo on p117) I looked like a junior version of Dracula, enough to put the frighteners on any but the most hardened of Fids. Pushing the boat out and whipping the engine into life was like starting out on a whole new trip, except this one was tinged with both regret and relief. Regret that this was the last major activity I was to carry out before leaving Signy for home, and relief that it was over without incident. With the RRS *John Biscoe* just out of Port Stanley en route to South Georgia, the first and only stop before Signy, all I had to do was pack up the multitude of specimens I'd collected, write up my notes and my final report, put my feet up and wait.

~~~

As I rounded North Point and headed across Borge Bay, the square speck of the base hut beckoned black against Factory Bluffs, which was powdered with the first of the autumnal snows. It may only have been a draught-ridden hole, but it was home and comfort, and hot meals, and even a hot bath. I wrinkled my nose at the odours that, mixed with the outboard fumes, reminded me vividly of a student visit to a knackers' yard: that combination of fresh and rotting blood and flesh mingled with the stench of half stewed bones. Did I really smell that bad? I rubbed my hand across my anorak sleeve, glistening oily in memory of all those Stinkers.

One sniff was enough. Even at six inches, my hand was pungency personified. Perhaps they could use it in the perfume industry, I mused. That brought a smile. After all, ambergris was highly prized and it was just balls of unextruded faecal matter that accumulated in the intestines of sperm whales. Eventually, the ambergris is found floating around in the oceans waiting to be picked up by the knowing, such as the Somali fishermen, who stake out territories on the beach and spend their lives waiting for the ambergris to float by. This is a family tradition; it was then, and is now, sold on to the perfume industry.

I looked at my hand, every nail, every crevice outlined in black as if in mourning. By God, I bet I'd clear the hut in ten seconds flat. That produced a guffaw. The tension of the last ten days alone was draining out of me. After so much effort – not merely struggling with Stinkers but constantly straining not to do something stupid and to survive – the unwinding process, the feeling of going home, was now taking over. It would be good to be back; to talk to others instead of myself; to eat real food (even if only out of a tin); to feel comfortably warm instead of uncomfortably cold; and to know I had survived and that the next step was homeward.

With half a mile or so to go, a sudden flurry of activity could be seen at base. Someone, indiscernible at that distance, came out and gazed hard in my direction, the low evening light gleaming on the short choppy waves making identification difficult. He disappeared and reappeared with what I took to be binoculars, and was joined by two others who, with hardly more than a glance, disappeared rapidly indoors.

As I got closer, another (or the same) figure appeared, strode down to the jetty, and hammered in what looked like a sign at the end of it. Others appeared and disappeared as rapidly. By the time I came alongside, all was silence: a face appeared momentarily in the sitting room window; it looked like George, grinning. After hitching up the dinghy I approached the sign. On it, hastily scrawled, were the words *No entry unless naked; strip here; we have run a bath.*

By now, several faces were to be seen behind the double glazing, grinning or holding their noses. I gave them the usual greeting, struggled out of my gear and shuffled inside, stark naked and suddenly weary. As I entered the long hall, I was greeted with slamming doors. I paused, and in the confined and somewhat warmer space, was hit with a wave of putrefying Petrel odours. I positively reeled.

I turned sharp left into the bathroom to be greeted with a half a bath full of steaming water. What luxury! Normally, baths were four or five inches deep, just enough to cover thighs – water collecting being a major chore. I peeled off the fetid underwear layers. The long johns and two string vests were highly odiferous; rigid with effluvium, they leaned drunkenly against the wall. After twenty minutes of absolute bliss, I dashed naked for the dormitory, for reasons of heat loss to vital parts more than for modesty.

~~~

Dressed and smelling sweetly, or so I imagined, I advanced on the kitchen, to be greeted with groans, growls and curses all attesting to the delicate aroma that still clung to me. The kindest, and least obscene, suggestion came from George, who said, 'You can fuck off and live in the emergency hut' – it was about a quarter of a mile away – 'until the boat comes. If you don't, I will.'

Having survived the onslaught, I wandered down to the bathroom to clear up, only to find that all my clothes had disappeared. A quick search and I discovered them fifty yards away on the beach downwind of the hut. There they remained, pegged out, until the boat arrived. Even though I had a great attachment to the anorak that I had worn in the field all winter and for two summers, I just couldn't bring myself to pack it, knowing that it, and probably I, would have been unceremoniously turfed out a porthole 'two-six' as the ex-Navy types would say, by my cabin companions.

By dinnertime, the exclamations of disgust had reduced to mostly mere murmurs of disapproval. The base diary summed it up: *Fergus was smelt coming around North Point. Emergency action taken to no avail.*

Leaving Antarctica: Hail and Farewell

Leaving Antarctica was even more exciting than arriving there. Suddenly, overnight, the RRS *John Biscoe* was there, unloading final winter stores and delivering last letters from family and friends for those of us coming out, and those staying on to winter at Signy. All the post was months old, but welcome nonetheless.

Tonsberg House was less *semper in excreta* than usual, a light dusting of snow covering up the many sins of omission: the tidy-up that ran out of steam with the rush of blood at the thought of leaving, of receiving mail, of seeing new faces, hearing new – or different – voices. Suddenly, a kaleidoscope of fresh images, to be stored up, to take out during the long winter nights, and to absorb overnight so that the first breakfast on board was among friends, or at least new acquaintances.

I spent the last night in the loft, up above the cacophony of new arrivals and more pints, blaring music, alcohol-induced heart-to-hearts, fun and gaiety. Macho and, as usual, inane comments about birds of various sizes and shades, whether dolly or otherwise, started up. Skirts were now above the knee! Chest-tensing, breath-gulping, scrotum-swelling tensions. I had left for Antarctica on 1 October 1957 and now, nearly three years later, I was finally going home.

Here in the loft with the ladder pulled up, I could contemplate the passage from full-time explorer to overnight has-been; no longer with a role, scientific or otherwise. Just one of a group enjoying a long jolly back to Blighty, to a fate less predictable, less certain, even unknown. To a world that had moved on by a litany of social, economic and political changes, the knowledge of which never penetrated the snow-driven sheets of ice crystals that had pulled a veil across Antarctica, frozen for the months and years past.

I would arrive home just as John F. Kennedy was running for presidency, the USA entered the Vietnam War and Beatlemania was taking over the world.

My mind floated extra-terrestrially. A special clarity cleared the way through clouds of atmospheric gases to a picture of a world, ice-covered at both ends and to the human ant colonies of the burgeoning Third World, as it was called then. China and India filled the screen, with Africa seemingly close behind, all striving to achieve what America, and to a much lesser extent Europe, had achieved at that time – like motor cars and fridges and radios for everyone.

Is that what I wanted? Is that what was needed for humanity to behave with humanity? The real focus had to be about survival. This, inevitably, was my primary concern. Every second, minute, hour, it was only a glance away. No matter what one was doing, whether climbing a snow-covered hill, skiing on the sea ice, spotting or potting birds and seals, or just staring at the frozen world of sea, ice and icebergs, survival was what it was all about. But how was I, we, surviving globally?

And what about the air we were breathing and its oxygen, central to the heart-regenerating internal systems? Would we run out of oxygen with the world population starting to go through the roof? Didn't the atmosphere have less than 25 per cent of water?

The plants of the world, on land and in the sea, would keep on producing oxygen if we kept on providing them with our waste carbon dioxide. What a good arrangement that was. Oxygen in, carbon dioxide out, and plants doing the reverse. What did we do before that happened? Who provided the carbon dioxide before we arrived on the planet? The dinosaurs? And before that? And before that again? It was only a hundred years since Darwin invented evolution and here we were – or at least some of us were – suggesting that evolving to our present state of wholeness had taken orders of magnitude longer than was generally believed; that the Flood was only yesterday; that Christianity was merely the newest fashion on the block.

But this was getting away from the bigger picture. How did we survive, through the multitudinous millennia with changing climates, freezing ice ages, intense tropical conditions and a world of dry deserts, now reduced to the Arctic, Antarctic and a few spots around the world, like the Sahara and the Kalahari?

Now with a wild bearded visage, hair down the back of my collar, face lined with deep cracks gouged by the wind and sun and baked hard by the frost, I wondered if friends and family would recognise me. I had left home a fresh-faced youth and was returning a soul-seared 24-year-old. I thought of burying myself up here in the loft under the pile of discarded clothes and ancient decrepit sleeping bags. Maybe no one would notice I was missing, and the ship would sail without me, and I would stow away for another winter. No need to confront the overtly polite questions of the family, who would listen to long-winded tales of the Antarctic with total incomprehension and rapidly fading interest.

And how would I cope with the three-year gaping gap in my knowledge of local and national events and personalities? What would, could, I talk about? Aside from familiar faces, would everything be a foreign land? I pulled myself down into the discarded pile and made a pillow of my sledging anorak, the one that had survived the winter, the stinking Stinkers and bloody seals, the one I was being forced to leave behind. At least my last contact with Antarctica would be a familiar one; to all intents and purposes it had become a part of my skin during the past fifteen months. A survival skin not so much cared for as cared about. I closed my eyes, the decibels below receded; tomorrow could look after itself.

~~~

At the second hoot of the ship's hooter, my eyes sprang open. Oh, shit, the effing *Biscoe* was off. I struggled out of the clothes pile. At least I was fully dressed, down to my Canadian hunting wellies, with their rubber feet and leather laced uppers, which I had scavenged from the shoe pile in another corner of the loft some weeks before when my one and only pair of ski boots finally disintegrated. One last look at my anorak – a caress of the wolverine-fringed hood – and I dashed down the loft, sprang open the loft ladder, hoping I didn't thump someone below, and sprinted out of the hut and down to the jetty.

There, the scow was waiting for the stragglers; I was not the only one. One last look at Tonsberg House from sea level and we were off. Five minutes later alongside the *Biscoe*, the hut and the few bodies gazing from the jetty already looked like a picture postcard, two-dimensional.

The cord maintaining and feeding the connections between the Fids and the Signy environment and ecosystem had been ruptured, never to be renewed. I stood at the aft rail, staring, wanting to fill my mind with all those last-minute images that I knew I would never see again. Soak up the vistas: Borge Bay, full of bergy bits, the icy crunch as the fringing reef of ice boulders pushed on the crest of the waves to add to the ice-littered shoreline, and the shrill screeching as the undertow forced some to retreat to the sea to await the next opportunity.

The engines groaned louder, pulsating, the deck vibrations sending a wave of tiny shivers up through my feet, my calves clenching, unused to the movements, swaying me off centre; pressure now on my right leg, now on the left. The five-degree gyration of the hull transmitting the message that we were at sea. The long passage from 60° south to 52° north was under way.

Now there was no turning back. Signy, the South Orkneys, Antarctica were all behind me. I waved a last farewell. Tiny jetty-bound figures waved back. This was their last contact with the outside world until the spring, at least seven long winter months away. That was my last contact with my safe haven, my home, my cocoon, my womb, my security for so long.

An ache was already developing for the long winter nights and the brilliant summer light. I walked to the aft rail. Tonsberg House and the wintering party were receding. Someone was walking up to Hut Point for a last wave, a last farewell.

As we rounded North Point, the hut and thousands of memories shrank to a dot and disappeared into the memory bank. Hut Point was the last visible feature of familiar ground: of home. A lone figure, tiny in the distance, stood there. I put up the binoculars, ever present. One of the new boys, Roger Filer, was my last glimpse of my last human connection to Signy, and he was to die tragically the following summer while banding Sheathbills at Gourlay, where I had trained him.

We headed out of Borge Bay, turning west around Coronation. I gazed at the horizon, a delicate frieze of distant icebergs flowing their solitary way north and east to their destination in the warmer waters of the cold temperate zone of the sub-Antarctic. We would be heading north by west for our last look at Port Stanley (and the governor's daughter).

I went below to the cabin I should have occupied the previous night. Drake's Passage was, as usual, a horrendous crossing. Fortunately, despite my lack of sea legs, I was OK; no vomiting from either end. Some of my fellow explorers were less fortunate, taking to their bunks for the duration, in between staggering to the heads (this was in the days before en suite – the

207

Biscoe was certainly no *Queen Elizabeth*).

This was my sixth time crossing Drake's Passage, and on every occasion the seas were less than kind; in fact, they were bloody awful. The ship leaned sideways onto the relentless rollers, pushed by the westerly winds of the circumpolar current: an awesome power that attacks the narrow gap between the tips of the Antarctic Peninsula and that of Tierra del Fuego, a mere 600 miles, with great ferocity. All the forces built up in the roaring forties and the ferocious fifties combined with the searing sixties. Then through Drake's Orifice with a relentless ferocity seen nowhere else on the planet. No wonder the Falklands was the graveyard of so many great ships beaten back from Cape Horn in the days of sail, to end up, if they were lucky, on the rocky shores of those islands.

~~~

But, once again, steam won out against the wind and waves of the Southern Ocean. We hove to in the sound facing Port Stanley less than forty-eight hours later, much to the relief of all. 'Thank God I don't have to do that effing trip ever again,' was the politest remark in the wardroom.

We all pushed and jostled as the gangplank was lowered and then the rush to get off, to feel terra firma under one's feet, to smell the difference between civilisation and a herd of, until very recently, sweaty ex-squaddies. Now they smelled of disinfectant soaps, scrubbed clean – more or less – hair mops combed for the first time in years, probably; some even with beards trimmed, the rest, wild-eyed with anticipation, crumpled clothes, washed but never ironed, pushing as if being off first was some sort of achievement and would win a prize. I swung around the inboard end of the metal gangplank, pushing and being pushed.

Here, mixed in with the motley crew of men were girls, women, mothers, all wearing dresses. Girls with *gúnas*, as we used to say in Irish, flashed into mind: white frocks, shorter than the normal school tartans; strong, brown, freckled legs; and tennis racquets. Here we were, silly grins plastered on our faces, delighted to be back in normal society even though all many of us could say was a tentative hello.

The locals were equally delighted at the influx of new faces. Being fed up of talking to the same people, the Kelpers were agog with the cacophony of new and different voices. Gradually, the fifty or so locals and the thirty or so soon-to-be-ex-Fids dispersed into smaller groups heading for houses, offices, shops or the only pub, to drink pints that weren't buffeted by wind or slopped by sea. Some made a beeline for the one and only shop worth visiting, the Falkland Island Company Store, to gaze at the amazing range of goods, clothes and cameras that were begging to be bought.

The healing effects of pastures new were the answer to old wounds. Put the aberrations of the past behind you and onward, Christian soldier, at least as far as the nearest pub, and for me a gallon of Coke. Is it conceivable in this day and age that any man could get to twenty-four and not ever have been pissed? Not even tipsy? That not a drop of alcohol had ever knowingly passed my lips – was I a saint or something? Could a society flourish with cohorts of young men – and even more women – who had pledged themselves never to let the evils of drink get hold of them? It says something for the power of the Irish Catholic Church that temperance was the Holy Grail, at least among the young in holy Ireland.

But the return to civilisation at Port Stanley, even if there was only the one street of any significance, was a blast. As we arrived, the signs went up à la Flanders and Swann, 'Lock up your daughters.' Everyone lined the jetty railings, muffled up in anoraks, scarves, gloves and woolly hats, confronting the bitter April winds blowing in straight from Cape Horn, only 400 miles away. The low mist shrouded the treeless landscape with an autumnal glow, the lines of houses with their higgledy-piggledy roofs outlined against the lowering sun.

And what did I do? I headed for the FIDS office to see if I could organise an outing to the penguin and seal colonies at Volunteers' Point. I barged into the office of the Colonial Secretary, keeper of the official lifeboat, who was keen to join the party. 'Would an early start be possible?' he enquired. My enthusiastic 'Yes!' caused a ripple of shock. 'Jolly good. Ten o'clock then, at the jetty.'

I smiled. Civilisation wasn't going to be so bad after all.

Epilogue.

Fergus O'Gorman believes he is the only surviving Irishman to have wintered in the Antarctic.

He was born in Dublin in 1934.

He was educated in O'Connell Schools in North Richmond St and graduated as a biologist from University College Dublin (UCD.)

His first job, after graduation, was as a research biologist for the British Antarctic Survey in Antarctica where he was stationed for three years from 1957 to 1960.

On his return from the Antarctic, from 1960-1962, he was research Fellow at Charing Cross Hospital Medical School.

In 1962, he returned to Ireland to lecture in University College Cork. (UCC)

His next appointment was as Scientific Adviser and Head of Research for the Irish Wildlife and National Parks Division of the Dept. of Lands and Forestry in Dublin.

He then became Head of Wildlife at the U.N (FAO) in Rome, and of the Wildlife Conservation Programme for the Mediterranean.

On his return to Ireland in 1972 he lectured in Trinity College Dublin and UCD, where he established the first World Heritage Management and Conservation Masters in Ireland.

He has a family of eight children, Tom, Fiona, Kevin, John, Aoife, AnneMarie, Stefanie and Ines.

Fergus' final journey to the Antarctic was with his partner Denise Comerford, in 2015. The Expedition of a Lifetime was organised to honour the 28 men and one woman who died while working for the British Antarctic Survey. Here Denise and Fergus had a Ceremony of Commitment on

Horseshoe Island, 68 degrees South, surrounded by penguins and seals (see photo page 124). Surely a fitting final chapter to Fergus' 'Antarctic Affair'.

Fergus and Denise live in Dalkey, Co. Dublin. Ireland

Acknowledgements

I owe a huge debt of thanks to all those who, over the years, encouraged me to keep on writing *Antarctic Affair* and to get to the end of this very long journey.

Most especially, my thanks to my partner, Denise, who over the past decade not only encouraged me, but also generously worked hard and continuously at getting my handwritten manuscript into its final shape.

And all the members of my extended family and especially my children, Tom, Fiona, Kevin, John, Aoife, AnneMarie, Stefanie and Ines, whose encouragement I relied on to keep going.

My thanks also to my publishers Angela Keogh and John MacKenna, of The Harvest Press, and Seamus Taaffe, chairman of the Shackleton Museum, Athy, Co. Kildare and the committee for supporting the publication of my book, *Antarctic Affair*.

Finally, it is my pleasure to thank Pat Falvey, the foremost Irish adventurer, whom I first met on a mountain, for all his prodding, kicking, and exhortations, which finally got the job done. His belief in my writing was essential.

Index

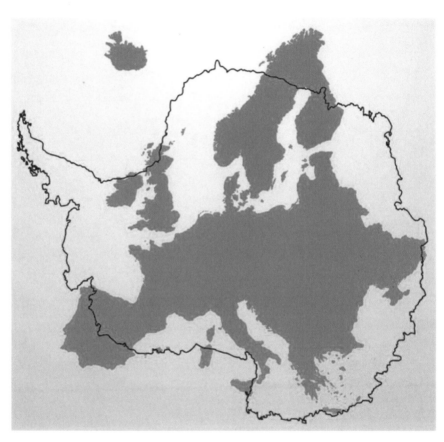

Comparing the size of Antarctica and Europe

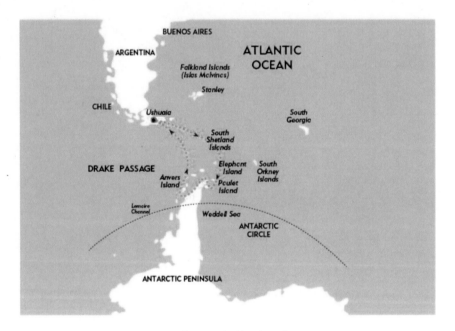

Antarctic Peninsula